County Clare
A History and Topography

Samuel Lewis

CLASP PRESS

CLASP PRESS
Clare County Library Headquarters,
Mill Road, Ennis, County Clare.

ISBN 1 900545 07 1
Paperback edition 1998

(ISBN 1 900545 00 4)
Hardback edition 1995

A History and Topography of County Clare
was originally published in 1837 as part of
A Topographical Dictionary of Ireland.

Cover design and illustration by Siobhan McCooey
from original engraving by Joseph Goodyear in
Lewis's Atlas comprising the counties of Ireland 1837.

This edition is limited to 1000 copies.

*CLASP wishes to acknowledge
the generous sponsorship of
Clare County Council,
and the invaluable assistance
and co-operation of
FAS, The Training Authority.
A special thanks to
Donal Griffin of FAS
for his encouragement and
enthusiasm for this project.*

Chairman's Introduction

Clare Local Studies Project (CLASP) was set up by members of the Clare Library staff to develop awareness of, and increase access to sources for local studies in Clare. Conscious of scarce resources, CLASP decided to link up with FAS, the Training Authority, so that its aims could be realised by co-operating with the training functions of FAS. This partnership has been working excellently since May 1995, and this publication is but one of a number of projects in hand at present. I should like to pay a particular tribute to Clare County Council, without whose generous sponsorship this publication would not have been possible.

As with any project of this nature, there are certain individuals who have played key roles in its development and implementation. Olivia Callinan, Project Supervisor, constituted the vital ingredient linking the talents and abilities of the trainees with the specialist skills of Anthony Edwards, the indexing skills of Maureen Comber, the background research of Pat Flynn and the artistic talent of Siobhan McCooey.

CLASP is an independent organisation consisting of Noel Crowley, Chairman; Ted Finn, Secretary; Anthony Edwards, Projects Officer & P.R.O.; Maureen Comber & Frances O'Gorman, Joint Treasurers. These are joined on the board by Martin Nolan and Peter Considine, M.C.C.

CLASP is a local organisation, using local talents and resources, for the benefit of the community..

Noel Crowley.

Acknowledgements

The trainees on the CLASP team began work on this publication in July 1995. They began by diligently sifting through all the parishes, towns and villages in Ireland, from the original publication by Samuel Lewis, and extracting every entry relevant to County Clare. This information was then entered into the computer, and the pains-taking task of proof reading the entire text kept the trainees occupied for some weeks.

I would sincerely like to congratulate and thank each trainee for their effort, dedication and co-operation in making this publication possible, namely, Mary Considine, Brid O'Gorman, Caroline Maloney, Kieran Murphy, Teresa Killeen, Irene Griffin, Michelle Galvin, Karen Liddane, Fionn Malone and especially Katie Fitzgerald, Mary MacNamara, Fiona Reddan and Jackie Dermody. I would also like to thank FAS for their assistance.

Finally I wish to acknowledge with gratitude and appreciation the expert advice, encouragement and assistance we received from Noel Crowley, Clare County Librarian; Anthony Edwards, Assistant Librarian, Clare County Library Headquarters; Maureen Comber and Deirdre Griffin, Local Studies Centre, Clare County Library. I am also grateful to Mr. Pat Flynn for his advice and assistance.

Olivia Callinan,
Project Supervisor.

PREFACE TO THE ORIGINAL

The publication of similar works on England and Wales, forming portions of a great national undertaking, intended to embrace Topographical Dictionaries of England, Wales, Ireland, and Scotland, had in some measure prepared the proprietors for the difficulties which they have encountered in their recent survey of Ireland. The numerous county histories, and local descriptions of cities, towns, and districts of England and Wales, rendered the publication of their former works, in comparison with the present, an easy task. The extreme paucity of such works, in relation to Ireland, imposed the necessity of greater assiduity in the personal survey, and proportionately increased the expense. But if the labour was thus augmented, the generous encouragement which the proprietors received animated them to a continuance of those exertions which have at length brought this portion of their undertaking to a close. To distinguish all to whom they are indebted for assistance in affording local information and facilitating their researches, would present a record of the names of nearly all the most intelligent resident gentlemen in Ireland : this fact, therefore, must be admitted as an apology for expressing, in a general acknowledgement, their gratitude for such disinterested services. They can with confidence assure their numerous subscribers, that, in the discharge of their arduous duties, they have unremittingly endeavoured to present every fact of importance tending to illustrate the local history, or convey useful information respecting the past or present state, of Ireland : fabulous tales and improbable traditions have generally been intentionally omitted ; the chief aim being to give, in a condensed form, a faithful and impartial description of each place.

To render the account of every town and place of importance as correct as possible, prior to its being finally put to press, proof sheets were forwarded to those resident gentlemen who had previously furnished local information, in order that, in their revisal of them, they might introduce any changes which had subsequently taken place, or improvements that might be at that time in progress : these were, with very few exceptions, promptly examined and returned, but in some instances inevitable delay was occasioned by the absence of the parties to whom they were addressed. Though this essential precaution may have retarded the publication, it has conduced materially to the accuracy of the work. For a similar reason, the time employed in the survey has been longer than was at first anticipated ; it having been thought advisable that the persons engaged in that arduous and important service should protract the period originally prescribed for their researches, rather than compromise the interests of the work by omitting to avail themselves of every possible source of intelligence.

The unsettled orthography of names rendered it somewhat difficult to select a standard of arrangement calculated to afford facility of reference. That mode of spelling was therefore adopted which, after careful examination and inquiry, appeared to be sanctioned by general usage ; and where a name was found to be spelt in two or more ways, a reference has been given from one to the other. On this head, two points may require explanation, as a guide to reference :- The final *l* in the prefix *Kill* has been dropped when followed by a consonant, and retained when followed by a vowel. The ultimate of the prefix *Bally* (a corruption of *Baile*) is written variously, the letter *i* being sometimes substituted for *y*, but the latter is by far the more general ; in respect to names compounded of this and other simple terms, the non-discovery of a place under the head *Bally* will lead to the inference that it is given as *Balli*.

It is necessary to state that all distances are given in Irish miles ; glebes, and every other extent of lands, except when otherwise expressed, in Irish plantation acres ; grants and sums of money, unless the standard be specified, may be generally regulated, as regards their amount, by the period to which they refer, in its relation to the year **1826**, when the assimilation of the currency took place. Numerous Reports to Parliament, of recent date, have been made available for supplying much useful statistical information. The Ordnance survey, so far as it has extended, has been adopted as the best authority for stating the number of acres which each parish comprises. As regards other parishes, the number of acres given is that applotted under the tithe composition act, which in some cases embraces the entire superficies of the parish, in others excludes an unproductive tract of mountain waste, of which the estimated value is too small to admit of its being brought under composition. The amount of parochial tithes was derived from parliamentary returns of the sums for which they have been compounded. In case of a union of parishes forming one benefice, and of which the incumbent only receives a portion of the tithes, the parishes constituting the benefice are enumerated under the head of that which gives name to it ; the tithes of the latter of which, and their application, are first stated ; then, the gross tithes of the benefice payable to the incumbent, the appropriation of the remaining portions of the tithes of the other parishes being detailed under their respective heads.

The census of **1831** has been adopted with reference to the population and number of houses ; and the Reports of the Commissioners on Ecclesiastical Revenue and Patronage, of Ecclesiastical Inquiry, and of Public Instruction, have furnished much valuable matter relative to the Church. The number of children educated in the several schools in connection with the Board of National Education is given from the Report of the Commissioners. With respect to other schools, the numbers are generally those reported by the Commissioners of Public Instruction, which, being the numbers entered upon the books of the different schools, must be regarded as exceeding those in actual attendance. In cases where the information obtained on the spot materially differed from that contained in the Reports, the former has been adopted ; but the introduction of the National system has caused such numerous alterations, as to render it extremely difficult to state with any degree of precision the exact number of children at present receiving instruction in each parish.

The Proprietors cannot indulge the hope that, in a work of such magnitude, containing notices so numerous and diversified, some errors may not be found : indeed, the information collected upon the spot, even from the most intelligent persons, has frequently been so contradictory, as to require much labour and perseverance to reconcile and verify it. They have, however, regardless of expense, used the most indefatigable exertions to attain correctness, and to render the work as complete as possible; and they, therefore, trust that occasional inaccuracies will receive the indulgence of the Subscribers. ___

Davoren, Basil, Esq., Henry-
street, Dublin, and Glenwood,
co. Clare

D'Esterre, R. Ker, Esq.,
Rossmanahir, co. Clare, and
George's-street, Limerick

Drew, Francis, Esq.,
Drewsborough, Scariff

Dyas, Capt. Joseph, Ennis

Elliott, John, Esq., M.D.,
Kilrush

Fahy, Very Rev. Charles, V.G.
& P.P., Tulla

Finucane, John, Esq.,
Ennistymon

Finucane, Michael, Esq.,
Stamer-park, Ennis

Fitz-Gerald, Augustine, Esq.,
Belmont, Miltown-Malbay

Fitzgerald, F. J., Esq., J.P.,
Adelphi, Corofin

Fitzpatrick, James, Esq., Capel-s
treet, Dublin, and Ennis

Fletcher, Robert B., Esq., C.C.P.,
Ennis

Fraser, James, Esq., M.D.,
Newmarket-on-Fergus

Furlong, Rev. Jonathan, R.C.C.,
Ennis

Gallery, Mr. E., Ennis

Geary, James, Esq., Kildysart

Gegan, Mr. Joseph, Ennis

Gibson, Peter, Esq., Ennis

Griffin, John, Esq., M.D.,
Kilrush

Hamilton, Samuel, Esq., M.D.,
Kilrush

Harley, John, Esq., Clonroad,
Ennis

Healy, Francis, Esq.,
Mogullane, Newmarket-on-
Fergus

Healy, Michael, Esq., M.D.,
Manus-house, Ennis

Hehir, Mr. Mort, Miltown
Malbay

Hickman, P., Esq., D.L. and
J.P., Kilmore, Knock

Hodges, George Crowe, Esq.,
Donogrogue-castle, Knock

Hogan, Edmund, Esq.,
Carahan-house, Ennis

Hunt, Robert, Esq., Oaklands,
Knock

Kean, William, Esq.,
Hermitage, Ennis

Keane, Robert, Esq., J.P.,
Beechpark, Ennis

Kelly, Matthew, Esq., Kilrush

Kennedy, Francis, Esq., Coppa-
lodge, Kilrush

Kenny, Edward, Esq., Roe-
house, Ennis

Kenny, Rev. John, V.G. and
P.P. of Kilrush

Kilfenora, The Very Rev. the
Dean of, Deanery,
Ennistymon

Killaloe, Clonfert, &c., The
Right Rev. Lord Bishop of

Kirby, Rev. John, P.P., St.
Catherine's Ennistymon

Luby, Rev. M.A., Ennis

Lucas, Rev. John, B.A., Kilrush

Lysaght, C. A., Esq.,
Rockforest, Corofin

Lysaght, George, Esq.,
Kilcorney, Burren, and
Glentworth-street, Limerick

Macbeth, John, Esq., Ennis

Mac Inorny, Rev. James, Clare

Mac Mahon, The Right Rev. P.,
D.D., R. C. Bishop of Killaloe

Mac Mahon, John, Esq.,
Firgrove-house, Bunratty
Mac Mahon, Patrick, Esq.,
Ennis
Macnamara, Francis, Esq., J.P.,
Arran-view, Ennistymon
Macnamara, J., Esq., Moher,
near Ennistymon
Macnamara, Major W. N., M.P.
and J.P., Doolin
McCulloch, Rev. Thomas,
M.A., Newmarket-on-Fergus
McDermott, William, Esq.,
M.D., Rose-cottage, Knock
McInerny, Rev. Thomas, P.P. of
Feakle, Tulla
McKennally, J., Esq., French-st.,
Dublin, and Crusheen, Ennis,
co. Clare
McMahon, Rev. M., P.P.,
Doonass
Mahon, Charles, Esq., J.P.,
Cahircalla, Ennis
Mahon, Edward, Esq.,
Newmarket-on-Fergus
Mahon, William R., Esq., J.P.,
New-park, Ennis
Malone, Rev. James, P.P. of
Doora
Malone, J. P., Esq., Killaloe
Malone, Rev. M., P.P., Cratloe,
near Limerick
Mangan, John, Esq., Gort, co.
Galway, and Ennis, co. Clare
Marrett, W. C., Esq., J.P.,
Square, Kilrush
Martin, Rev. James, A.B., J.P.,
Kilmurry-glebe, Knock
Meehan, Terence, Esq., Ennis
Menzies, James, Esq., Ennis
Miller, Captain, J.P., Ennis
Molony, James, Esq., J.P.,
Kiltanon, near Tulla
Moran, John S., Mucknish,
Burrin

Morony, F. G., Esq., J.P.,
Seaview, Miltown-Malbay
Morony, John, Esq., Westpark,
Miltown-Malbay
Morony, T. H., Esq., J.P.,
Limerick, and Miltown-house,
co. Clare
Murphy, Mr. Edward, Killaloe

Nelley, Rev. Michael, P.P.,
Ennistymon
Nisbett, Rev. R. W., A.M.,
O'Gonnelloe-glebe, Killaloe

O'Brien, Cornelius, Esq., J.P.,
Birchfield
O'Brien, Sir E., Bart., J.P.,
Dromoland, Newmarket-on-
Fergus
O'Brien, George, W., Esq.,
M.D., Ennis
O'Brien, Jeremiah, Esq.,
Ryninch, Killaloe
O'Brien, John, Esq., Elmvale
O'Brien, Lucius, Esq.,
Dromoland
O'Brien, Rev. M., P.P.,
Kilkeedy, Corofin
O'Brien, Stafford, Esq., J.P.,
Cratloe-woods, co. Clare, and
Blatherwycke-park,
Northamptonshire
O'Brien, W., Esq.,
Rossmanagher-cottage, Six-
mile-bridge
O'Callaghan, Rev. Denis, P.P. of
Carron, near Corofin
O'Callaghan, George, Esq.,
Mary-fort, Tulla
O'Grady, Daniel, Esq., J.P.,
Shore-park, Kildysart
O'Loghlen, Hugh, Esq., J.P.,
Port
O'Loghlen, Ryan, Esq.,
Rockview, Ennis

O'Shaughnessy, The Very Rev. Terence, R.C. Dean of Killaloe, and P.P. of Ennis

Paterson, Irvin W., Esq., Cottage, Kilrush
Paterson, W. F., Esq., Newmarket-on-Fergus
Powell, Edmund, Esq., Fountain, Ennis
Powell, P., Esq., Poplar, Corofin
Powell, Thomas, Esq., Newmarket-on-Fergus
Purdon, S. G., Esq., J.P., Tincrana, Killaloe

Quin, Rev. Andrew, P.P., Kilfenora

Reade, Edward, Esq., Kilrateera, Scariff
Reade, Philip, Esq., J.P., Wood-park, Scariff
Reddan, Matthew, Esq., Shannon-view, Scariff
Ryan, Jos., Esq., O'Briery-bridge

Sampson, Denis, Esq., St. Catherines, Scariff, and St. Stephen's-green, co. Clare
Scott, John, Esq., J.P., Cahiracon, Kildysart
Sheehan, A., Esq., Ennis
Sheehan, Rev. John, P.P., Killeilagh
Singleton, John, Esq., J.P., Quinville-abbey, Quin
Stacpoole, Andrew, Esq., J.P., Ballyally, Ennis
Stacpoole, Richard, Esq., Ennis
Stacpoole, R. J., Esq., D.L., J.P., Eden-vale, Ennis
Stamer, John, Esq., Clare-castle

Steele, Thomas, Esq., Lough O'Connell, Ennis
Studdert, George, Esq., J.P., Clonderlaw, Knock
Studdert, Jonas, Esq., Riverston, Corofin
Studdert, Jonas, Esq., J.P., Atlantic-lodge, Kilkee
Studdert, Joseph G., Esq., Woodlawn, Knock
Studdert, Rev. Richard, A.B., Quin- glebe
Studdert, Richard, Esq., Kilrush
Studdert, W., Esq, Thornbury, Knock

Tallent, Rev. Edward, R.C.C., Knock
Townsend, Henry, Esq., Ennis
Trousdell, Richard, Esq., Forte, Kilrush
Trousdell, Rev. Henry, A.B., Kilkeady-glebe, Corofin
Tully, Lieut. John, R.N., Killaloe

Unthank, Robert S., Esq., Marine-villa, Kilrush

Vallancey, Richard, Esq., Killaloe
Vandeleur, Crofton M. Esq., J.P., Kilrush-house

Walker, C., Esq., Woodfield, Broadford, co. Clare, and Limerick
Walsh, Rev. Stephen, P.P. of Rath and Kilnaboy, Corofin
Watson, James, Esq., Millbrook, Killaloe
Westropp, Capt. H., Newlawn, Tulla

Introduction

In 1837, Samuel Lewis issued his *A Topographical Dictionary of Ireland*. This valuable work was published in two volumes running to over 1400 pages and aimed to

present every fact of importance tending to illustrate the local history, or convey useful information respecting the past and present state, of Ireland (and) to give, in a condensed form, a faithful and impartial description of each place.

Arranged in discrete alphabetical entries - starting, incidentally, with the parish of Abbey, in Clare - we find accounts of cities, towns and villages, particulars of dioceses, parishes and counties, and short references to coastal and other islands. All in all, it presents a wonderful gazetteer of the whole of Ireland, providing much background information to the past and, perhaps more importantly, permitting us to glimpse facets of life as it was prior to the Famine. While making use of official and other publications, it is obvious from the Preface that the publishers were, in no small way, indebted for local information to material supplied by "the most intelligent resident gentlemen in Ireland." A list of subscribers with Clare addresses among the almost two thousand who pre-paid for their copies of the two-volume work, is also included in this publication. No doubt this list contains many of the above "intelligent resident gentlemen".

As might be expected, original copies of the original two-volume edition are now a rarity and command high prices on the antiquarian book market. An American reprint publisher brought out an edition some time ago, but even that is beyond the reach of most buyers. In bringing together in one short volume all the Clare entries it was felt that a service has been rendered to readers in the county and makes available in an accessible form material which might otherwise have been out of reach.

The Clare entries given here are taken as they appear in the original. No attempt has been made to "improve" or correct: Lewis himself refers to the "unsettled orthography of names" and the spelling used in the text has been faithfully followed. The "corrected" forms adopted by the Ordnance Survey have not been imposed as will be readily seen in regard to a number of parishes and several towns. Perhaps it should be pointed out that the parish entries refer to the then parishes of the Established Church and not to the Civil Parishes, which though conterminous with the former will be found, particularly after the Ordnance Survey was completed, to have been somewhat "tidied up". The civil Parish of O'Briensbridge is treated under the entry for Killaloe, while both Inagh and Ruan have been subsumed in Dysert. While many parishes still have detached portions, nestling in adjoining ones, the impression given by Lewis is of many more. An added confusion in Lewis' *Dictionary* is the occasional assigning to two different neighbouring parishes of gentlemen's seats or houses. There are two parish entries which owe their inclusion more to precedent than to actuality: Innisdadrom may have had a separate existence as a benefice but geographically it forms part of Clondagad: Donamona, stated to be in the barony of Tulla and merged with Killaloe, is, in fact, another "lost" parish on the other side of the Shannon, and not in Clare at all. At the time Lewis' *Dictionary* was compiled, Inniscaltra was only partly in Clare. However since the 1898 Local Government Act it is now wholly in this county. Additionally, the parish of Clonrush, formerly in Galway, has been added to Clare. The relevant entry and that for Mountshannon have been shown here as addenda.

In, total, Lewis' *Dictionary*, runs to over 1400 pages. As each page is double-columned and contains 64 lines of type to the column, it hardly comes as a surprise that the entire text exceeds one-and-a-half million words. The Clare entries, which are abstracted here, total over 50,000 words, and fall into the categories previously mentioned. The longest distinct article deals, as one might expect, with the county as a whole: there are 79 entries on parishes, 43 on towns and villages, eight on islands, and several single line entries, either directing one's attention to another entry or giving an alternative name for some location. References to the relevant dioceses are incorporated into the main account of both Killaloe and Kilfenora: though three parishes belong to the Diocese of Limerick (Killeely, St. Munchin's and Kilquane or St. Patrick's).

The Clare County section firstly gives details of the location, area and population, followed by a short historical account. Then comes a fairly comprehensive account of the ecclesiastical and civil divisions, with descriptions of local government, the courts, police and various county establishments, such as the house of industry, the infirmary etc. Thereafter follows a physical description and some information on the climate and soils. The agriculture of the county is next outlined in some detail, after which comes an account of the limited industrial activity. What would now be described as the infrastructural system is then dealt with i.e. roads, navigation and communications. Finally, after considering the remains of antiquity we get an all too short account of the social aspects of life. It is perhaps gratifying that there is a passing reference to the game of hurling.

The parish entries follow a somewhat similar, though necessarily abbreviated, format to that of the county. A general description precedes details on such items as fairs and markets, roads, ruins, schools, and churches, the gentlemen's seats within the parish, and, invariably, details of the status of the Established Church with a brief allusion to the R. C. division. If there are any natural curiosities or if the locality is associated with some famous person, this is often mentioned. Inevitably the quality and extent of the information provided, varies from parish to parish. In some cases what we are told is tantalisingly brief, while in other instances one feels that the local correspondent has engaged in a 'puffing' exercise to give added importance to his chosen place.

With regard to the accounts of towns and villages a suspicion that something similar is afoot suggests itself. We have noticed that in all some forty-three such places are given separate entries for the county as a whole. Surprisingly, over a quarter (twelve, in fact) are located within the barony of Burren. However, it should be pointed out that all of these were given the status of village or hamlet in the 1831 Census and may well have been included for this reason. On the other hand, there are a number of entries which did not attain that status in the Census but which, by 1841, recorded substantial populations: Carrigaholt, Ballynacally and O'Callaghan's Mills have been noticed in Lewis' *Dictionary* but were seemingly, overlooked by the enumerators in the 1831 Census. Perhaps there is a lesson here - all sources of information bear scrutiny.

Naturally, there are flaws in Lewis' *Dictionary*, and, here and there, errors can be detected, but these are generally of a minor nature, reflecting the current knowledge of the time. In the area of antiquarian study, for instance, describing the Romanesque doorway at Dysert as a 'richly sculptured Saxon arch' or referring to ring-forts as 'Danish' forts or, for that matter, applying the term 'cromlech' to a variety of megalithic remains is simply using the expressions then in vogue. Assigning the ruins of the church at Kilshanny to the Cistercians ('a cell to the abbey of Corcomroe') rather than to the Augustinians was an error which persisted long after Lewis' time. Under the heading Feacle, we get the information that this parish extends to the 'confines of the county of Limerick', when, of course, it should be the county of Galway. Such obvious mistakes are, thankfully, few and far between. However in the entry for Carrigaholt we are told of '500 Currachs', which seems highly unlikely.

For modern readers, the seemingly disproportionate amount of space given to the nitty-gritty of the Established Church organisation may well seem at odds with that church's minority role among the population at large. However, one must remember that Lewis' readership would be largely drawn from that community and that, effectively, this church was (until disestablishment in 1869) a recognised arm of State. The ecclesiastical details provided do serve an unwitting purpose, in that they reflect the economy of the pre-Reformation Church, which was scrupulously adopted by the new reformed organisation. The retention of appurtenances like the 'parishes' of Donamona and Inisdadrom referred to earlier are cases in point. The convoluted nature of rectories and vicarages reflect an earlier age too as, indeed, does the whole question of patronage and improprietorship, so assiduously dealt with.

One wishes that as much concern had been directed at some of the more mundane developments taking place in the 1830's. Tithes may have been a contentious issue then but there were other matters of moment which are not mentioned. Nevertheless it is possible to discern that upsurge in church building, which was such a feature of Catholic life in the last century. It will be seen from Lewis' *Dictionary* that this was not so much a phenomenon that followed Emancipation but dates from the relaxation of the Penal Laws at the close of the previous century. Church building at this period was not confined to the Catholics: the Protestant church at Clonlara was added to in 1831, while a new church for Kilmanaheen replaced the old in the same year. Likewise, the provision of glebe-houses in different parishes is noted. The embryonic tourist business is noticed in Kilkee, Lahinch and Spanish Point and it was felt that in the parish of Abbey 'the coast is well adapted for sea bathing'. We also come across a passage in the entry for Kilmoon which proved to be prophetic: Several cottages have, however, been recently built in the vicinity of these waters (the wells of Lisdoonvarna) for the reception of visiters: and if the proprietor continues his improvements, and a facility of access be afforded, this place will probably become one of the most frequented spas in Ireland.

'Facility of access' would appear to have been of much concern to Lewis and there are frequent references to new lines of road. That from 'the newly erected Wellesley bridge at Limerick' to Cratloe is noted, as, indeed are many others such as the road along the shore of Lough Derg, between Killaloe and Scariff.

In a different sense, Lewis' *Topographical Dictionary* itself permits the present-day reader a degree of 'facility of access' to those times immediately before the Famine. Some of the themes dealt with, have been touched upon here. Obviously there are more: the reader is invited to prise them out for him or herself.

Pat Flynn

ABBEY, a parish and village, in the barony of **BURREN**, county of **CLARE**, and province of **MUNSTER** ; containing, with the post-town of Burren, 2493 inhabitants, of which number, 128 are in the village. This place, which is situated on the shores of the harbour of Burren in the bay of Galway, and on the road from Galway to Ennistymon, derives its name from an ancient Cistertian abbey founded here, either by Donald O'Brien, King of Limerick, in 1194, or by his son Donough Carbrac O'Brien, in the year 1200. This establishment, designated the abbey of Corcomroe, Corcomruadh, or *De Petra fertili*, and called also Gounamonagh, or "the Glen of the Monks," is said to have been a sumptuous edifice, dedicated to the Blessed Virgin, and dependent on or connected with the abbey of Suire, or Innislaunaght, in the county of Tipperary : it was afterwards made subject to the celebrated abbey of Furness, in Lancashire, and had a cell annexed to it in Kilshanny, in the adjoining barony of Corcomroe. The remains are extensive, forming an interesting object as seen from the road, and presenting evident traces of its former splendour : a fine pointed arch is still tolerably perfect, and is particularly admired for the beauty of its proportions ; and there are some remains of the stately tomb of the King of Thomond, who was killed in a battle fought near this place, in 1267. The parish extends along the southern shore of the bay, on the confines of the county of Galway, and comprises 5545 statute acres, as applotted under the tithe act. The greater portion is under tillage ; the land along the coast produces good crops of wheat, but that in the interior is hilly and unproductive, adapted only for grazing ; the system of agriculture has been greatly improved through the exertions of Burton Bindon, Esq., and Messrs. Hynes and Moran. There are some limestone quarries of excellent quality, and sea manure is found in abundance on the shore. The principal seats are Finvarra House, the residence of - Skerret, Esq. ; and Curranroe, of Burton Bindon, Esq. The small port of New Quay is situated about a quarter of a mile to the north of the village of Burren ; a constant intercourse is kept up with Galway, on the opposite side of the bay, and a considerable trade in corn and fish is carried on ; the boats employed in the Galway bay fishery rendezvous here, and more than 100 of them have at one time taken shelter in stormy weather. The port affords great facilities for commerce, as vessels of considerable burden can approach at any time of the tide : the coast is well adapted for sea bathing. The great oyster bed, called the Red Bank, to the east of Burren, and said to be one of the most extensive on the Irish coast, was established some years since by Mr. Bindon, and is now in great celebrity : it is stocked with young oysters, chiefly from Connemara, aud more than 150 persons, chiefly women and children, are regularly employed. A considerable trade is also carried on in sea-weed with the farmers of the interior, which has been greatly increased since the construction of a new line of road from this place leading through the parishes of Kinvarra and Killeny, in the county of Galway, and of Kilkeady and Inchicronan, in the county of Clare. The harbour of New Quay, or Burren, called also Curranroe, is one of the several inlets of the bay of Galway : it lies to the south of Aughnish Point, and extends four miles up to Curranroe Bridge. The late Fishery Board built a small quay in the narrow part of the channel, at the village of New Quay (so called from the construction of this quay, about eight years since), a little to the east of an older one, of which there are still some remains : vessels of 100 tons' burden can come close up to it and deliver their cargoes. A court is held at Burren by the seneschal of the manor, about once in six weeks, for the recovery of small debts. The parish is in the diocese of Kilfenora, and is a rectory, partly without provision for the cure of souls : the tithes, with the exception of those of the townlands of Aughnish, Finvarra, Behagh, and Kilmacrane, which are annexed to the parish of Kilcorney, are impropriate in Pierse Creagh, Esq., and amount to £120. In the R. C. divisions it is the head of a union or district, comprising also the parish of Oughtmanna ; the chapel is situated in the village of Behagh, and it is intended to establish a school connected with it. There is a pay school, in which are about 30 boys and 15 girls. On the summit of Rosraly mountain is a well springing from the solid rock ; it is dedicated to St. Patrick, and produces water of the purest quality, which is conveyed by pipes to the road side at the foot of the mountain.-See **BURREN**.

ARDSALLIS, a village, in the parish of **TOMFINLOUGH**, barony of **BUNRATTY**, county of **CLARE**, and province of **MUNSTER**, 51/2 miles (N. W.) from Six-mile-bridge, on the road from Newmarket-on-Fergus to Quin : the population is returned with the parish. Nearly adjoining it is a good race-course, which was formerly much frequented, but the races have been for many years discontinued. Fairs are held on the 12th of May and the 12th of August, chiefly for cattle, and were formerly well attended.

AUGHNISH, a village, in a detached portion of the parish of **OUGHTMANNA**, barony of **BURREN**, county of **CLARE**, and province of **MUNSTER**, 5 miles (N. W.) from Burren ; containing 46 houses and 304 inhabitants. This village, like others on this part of the coast, is frequented during the summer for sea-bathing; it is situated on the bay of Galway and near Aughnish Point, a headland on the north side of the harbour of New Quay, projecting into the bay from the peninsula formed by the parish of Duras, in the county of Galway, and forming the northern extremity of the county of Clare. On this point is a martello tower, and there is also one on Finvarra Point, to the south-west, in another detached portion of the parish.

BALLINACALLY, a village, in the parish of **KILCHRIST**, barony of **CLONDERLAW**, county of **CLARE**, and province of **MUNSTER**, 3 miles (N. N. E.) from Kildysart ; the population is returned with the parish. It is situated on the road from Kildysart to Ennis, and near the river Fergus, on the banks of which is a small quay of rude construction, from which corn, butter, pork, and other agricultural produce are sent to Limerick, in boats of 10 or 12 tons burden, and where limestone and sea manure are landed for the supply of the neighbourhood. It has a daily penny post to Ennis and Kilrush, and a public dispensary : and fairs are held on June 14th, Sept. 16th, and Nov. 8th, chiefly for cattle. A little to the north of the village is the ruined tower or castle of Dangan, the upper part of which is supported only by the winding stone staircase.-See **KILCHRIST**.

BALLYCONREE, a hamlet, in the parish of **DROMCREHY**, barony of **BURREN**, county of **CLARE**, and province of **MUNSTER** ; containing 9 houses and 60 inhabitants.

BALLYNACRAGGY, a hamlet, in the parish of **DROMCREEHY**, barony of **BURREN**, county of **CLARE**, and province of **MUNSTER**, 3 miles (W.) from Burren ; containing 19 houses and

123 inhabitants. This place, which derives its name from an ancient castle, of which there are some remains, is situated on the road from Burren to Ballyvaughan. A school is about to be established, for which purpose Captain Kirwan has given the site and £10 towards the erection of the building.-See **DROMCREEHY**.

BALLYVAUGHAN, a village, in the parish of **DROMCREEHY**, barony of **BURREN**, county of **CLARE**, and province of **MUNSTER**, 6 miles (W.) from Burren ; containing 151 inhabitants. This place is situated on a small bay to which it gives name on the western coast, and opening into the bay of Galway. The village, in 1831, contained 23 houses, since which time several new houses have been built, and it is progressively improving. Some of the inhabitants are employed in the herring fishery, which is carried on successfully on this coast. The bay is very shallow and in general fit only for boats ; but small vessels may anchor in 2 1/2 fathoms of water on good holding ground, about two or three cables' length south of Finvarra Point. There are some remains of an old quay, which is now of little use ; a new quay would add greatly to the prosperity of the place, as, independently of the fishery, turf is landed here in great quantities from Connemara for the supply of the neighbouring country. A market for corn and pigs is held weekly on Thursday; and fairs have been lately established on the 24th of June and 23rd of September. Here is a station of the constabulary police ; also a coast-guard station, which is one of the seven that constitute the district of Galway. A court for the manor of Burren is held by the seneschal about once in six weeks, at which small debts are recoverable ; and the road sessions for the district are also held in the village. At a small distance to the east, and near the shore, are some vestiges of the old castle of Ballyvaughan.-See **DROMCREEHY**.

BEHAGH, or **BEAGH**, a hamlet, in the parish of **ABBEY**, barony of **BURREN**, county of **CLARE**, and province of **MUNSTER** ; containing 14 dwellings and 101 inhabitants. The parochial R. C. chapel, a small thatched building, is situated here.

BROADFORD, a post-town, in the parish of **KILSEILY**, barony of **TULLA**, county of **CLARE**, and province of **MUNSTER**, 8 miles (N.) from Limerick, and 94 miles (S. W. by W.) from Dublin; containing 71 houses and 383 inhabitants. It is picturesquely situated on the road from Killaloe to Ennis, at the foot of a range of hills extending to Lough Derg on the Shannon, and has a post-office dependant on that of Limerick ; a constabulary police force is stationed here, and fairs are held on the 21st of June and the 21st of November. The parish church, a neat building with a square tower, is situated in the town ; and a large and handsome R. C. chapel is now in course of erection on an eminence overlooking it. Here are the parochial school, (chiefly supported by the minister) and a public dispensary. This place is much visited by anglers and sportsmen : the neighbourhood affords excellent grouse shooting, and about a mile to the west is Doon lake, remarkable for the size of its pike, and abounding also with bream. In the vicinity are several gentlemen's seats and shooting-lodges, which are more particularly noticed in the article on Kilseily. There are some excellent quarries near the village, producing slate of superior quality.-See **KILSEILY**.

BUNRATTY, a post-town, and parish, in the barony of **BUNRATTY**, county of **CLARE**, and province of **MUNSTER**, 6 miles (W. by N.) from Limerick, and 100 miles (W. S. W.) from Dublin ; containing 1300 inhabitants. This place is situated on the mail coach road from Limerick to Ennis, and on the northern shore of the river Shannon. The castle was erected in 1277, by the De Clares, and was subsequently the residence of the Earls of Thomond ; it was besieged in 1305, but not taken ; and the small town adjacent to it was burned in 1314. The castle was either enlarged or rebuilt by Sir Thomas de Clare, in 1597, and is still the largest in the county. Till within the last few years it was the residence of T. de Clare Studdert, Esq., who has erected a handsome modern mansion in the demesne, and the old castle is now used as a constabulary police barrack. It is a lofty and massive quadrangular structure, with a tower at each angle ; the upper parts of the towers at each end of the quadrangle are connected by an arch ; it still retains its old baronial hall unaltered, and, till deserted by the family, displayed a spacious and lofty banqueting-room ; the outworks and appendages were of great extent, as is evident from the vestiges that may still be

5

traced. A handsome bridge of one arch was built over the river Ougarnee, by Mr. Studdert, who also constructed near it a commodious quay, which is about to be enlarged ; boats of large size can come up to it. Considerable quantities of sea manure are landed here for the supply of the neighbourhood, and turf is brought from Kilrush. In the Shannon near this place are several islands, one of which, called Quay Island, is inhabited by only one family : the anchorage off this island, called Bunratty Roads, is considered to be the best in the Shannon, and here the West India vessels discharge their cargoes for Limerick. Off Clonmoney is another island, called Saints' Island, containing about 50 statute acres of the richest land, and inhabited by two families. Fairs are held here on Feb. 3rd, the second Tuesday before Easter, June 3rd, July 19th, and Oct. 20th, for cattle, pigs, and sheep. A seneschal's court for the manor of Bunratty is occasionally held, in which debts not exceeding £10 late currency may be recovered.

The parish comprises 2649 statute acres, as applotted under the tithe act, and mostly in pasture ; those parts bordering on the Shannon afford rich grazing land. Bunratty Castle, the seat of T. de Clare Studdert, Esq., is pleasantly situated within the ancient demesne, and commands fine views of the Shannon and of an extensive tract of country : the mansion is spacious and of modern design, and the demesne is embellished with fine timber of stately growth. Immediately adjoining the village is Bunratty, the residence of Mrs. Paliser, in the rear of which are the ruins of an old church, the walls of which are in good preservation. The other seats are Clonmoney, that of D. Canny, Esq., and Woodpark, of M. Dalton, Esq. It is a rectory and vicarage, in the diocese of Killaloe ; the rectory forms part of the union of Tomfinlogh or Traddery, in the patronage of the Earl of Egremont; and the vicarage part of the union of Kilfinaghty. The tithes amount to £150, of which £100 is payable to the rector, and £50 to the vicar. The church of the union is at Six-mile-bridge, in that parish. The glebe-house is situated on a glebe of 11 acres in this parish, subject to a rent of £21. 10. per annum late currency. In the R. C. divisions it forms part of the union or district of Newmarket, and is held with several others by the administrator of the R. C. Bishop of Killaloe ; the chapel is a commodious modern building. There is a small school under the superintendence of the vicar, in which are about 20 children ; and at Clonmoney is a school under the direction of the R. C. clergyman. There is also a private school, in which about 65 children are educated.

BURREN, or **BURRIN**, a village and post-town, in the parish of **ABBEY**, barony of **BURREN**, county of **CLARE**, and province of **MUNSTER**, 18 miles (N. by W.) from Ennis, and 115 3/4 miles (W. by S.) from Dublin : containing 23 houses and 147 inhabitants. This place is situated on the road from Ballyvaughan to Curranroe Bridge, and about a quarter of a mile from the small harbour of Burren, now called New Quay, from the construction of a quay within the last few years, a little to the east of the former, of which there are still some remains : it is a constabulary police station. A court is held every six weeks by the seneschal of the manor, in which small debts are recoverable. The harbour is frequented by 30 hookers of about 12 tons' and 150 yawls of 3 tons' burden each, engaged in the fishery, which affords employment to about 500 men. Large quantities of corn, butter, sheep, and pigs, are shipped here ; and such is the convenience of the harbour, that in hard weather 100 sail of small craft have taken refuge in it at a time. The coast is noted for its oysters, which are in high repute for their superior flavour and quality ; the great oyster bed, called the Burren Red bank, and the harbour, are more particularly described in the account of the parish of Abbey, *which see.*

CALLAGHAN'S MILLS, a village, in the parish of **KILLURANE**, barony of **TULLA**, county of **CLARE**, and province of **MUNSTER**, 3 miles (S.W.) from Tulla : the population is returned with the parish. It is situated on the high road from Six-mile-bridge to Scariff, and about midway on the road from Tulla to Broadford. Fairs are held on May 8th, June 27th, and Nov. 14th. Here is a R. C. chapel of ease to the parochial chapel of Kilkishen, in which a school is also held under the superintendence of the curate.

CANON ISLAND, or **INNISNEGANANAGH**, an island, in the parish of **KILDYSART**, barony of **CLONDERLAW**, county of **CLARE**, and province of **MUNSTER**, about 1 1/2 mile (E.) from Kildysart : the population is returned with the parish. It is situated at the confluence of the Shannon and Fergus, about 3/4 of a mile from the shore, and contains 207 acres of excellent land, partly under tillage, the sea-weed collected on its shores being used as manure. It was anciently called *Elanagranoch* ; and here Donald O'Brien, king of Limerick, in the 12th century, founded or rebuilt a priory for Canons Regular of the order of St. Augustine. A moiety of the priory, with the various lands, tithes, profits, and demesne lands thereof, was granted in fee, in 1605, to Donogh, Earl of Thomond, and was afterwards granted in fee, or confirmed, to his successor, Henry, in 1661. The ruins, which are situated at the north-eastern extremity of the island, consist of a square tower and a considerable portion of the body of the building, which is said to have covered a quarter of an acre.

CARRIGAHOLT, a small port and village, in the parish and barony of **MOYARTA**, county of **CLARE**, and province of **MUNSTER**, 11 3/4 miles (W.) from Kilrush : the population is returned with the parish. It is situated on the harbour and road-stead of the same name, within the estuary of the river Shannon. The castle, now in ruins, was formerly the fortified residence of the Mac Mahons, the chiefs of that part of this country which forms the peninsula called the "Western Corkavaskin," still denominated "the west." The last siege to which it was exposed was in 1649, when it was taken by Gen. Ludlow, and Teigue Keigh was the last of the Mac Mahons to whom it belonged. On his attainder it passed by grant from Queen Elizabeth to Henry O'Brien, brother to the Earl of Thomond, whose unfortunate grandson, Lord Clare, resided in it when he raised a regiment of horse, called the "Yellow Dragoons," which in 1689 was the flower of King James's army. The town now belongs to Lady Burton, whose ancestor was an officer in the army of King William. The ruins of the castle occupy a bold situation on the verge of a cliff overhanging the sea, enclosed by a court-yard and high walls on one side, and by rocks and the bay on the other. A small quay or pier was constructed partly by the late Fishery Board and partly by grand jury presentments : it is of considerable service to agriculture and the fisheries, and is frequented by six hookers, of seven tons each, and upwards of 500 corrachs, which give employment to about 400 persons, particularly in the herring fishery, which commences in July. This is the principal place in the neighbourhood for the shipment of agricultural produce ; 900 tons of grain, 700 firkins of butter, and 3000 pigs, having lately been shipped here in one year, by three individuals : it also exports hides to Limerick. The bay of Carrigaholt lies opposite that part of the Kerry shore, within the mouth of the Shannon, which is called the Bale bar. It has good and secure anchorage with the wind to the northward of west, but being entirely exposed to the ocean swell, the sea, which sets in with southerly or westerly winds, renders it unsafe to lie there. The inner harbour, however, is better protected from those winds, but is shallow, having no more than $2_{1/2}$ or 3 fathoms of water within the line from Carrigaholt Castle to the opposite side of the bay. Capt. Manby, who was employed by the Irish Government to survey the Shannon, recommended that a small pier should be extended from the spot called Lord Clare's pier, (which was formed in 1608 but has gone to decay,) at nearly a right angle to the shore, sufficiently to afford shelter to the one that already exists, and that this should be carried out farther, so as to permit boats to sail from it till almost low water. The roads in the immediate vicinity of the village are in bad condition, and must be repaired before the port can be easily accessible by land. The valley on the northside of Kilkadrane Hill having been often mistaken by night for the proper channel for entering the Shannon, a light has been placed on the top of the hill, red to seaward, and a fixed bright light as seen descending the river. In the village is a public dispensary, and near it is the R. C. chapel.- See **MOYARTA**.

CARRUNE, CARRON, or **CARNE**, a parish, in the barony of **BURREN**, county of **CLARE**, and province of **MUNSTER**, 6 miles (N. N. W.) from Curofin ; containing 1045 inhabitants. It is situated on the road from Ennis and Curofin to Burren and New Quay, and is chiefly rocky pasture well adapted for sheep, of which the farmers' stock principally consists ; a very small proportion is under tillage, which is slowly improving. Limestone abounds, and some copper mines were formerly worked, but are now discontinued. Columbkill Cottage, the neat residence of Terence O'Brien, Esq., and Tarmon parsonage, recently erected for the R. C. clergyman, are the only seats of importance. The living is a rectory and vicarage, in the diocese of Kilfenora ; the rectory constitutes part of the sinecure union of Killielagh, in the patronage of the Marquess of Thomond ; and

9

the vicarage is part of the union of Noughaval, and the corps of the precentorship of the cathedral church of St. Fachnan, Kilfenora, in the patronage of the Bishop. The tithes amount to £70 per annum, of which one-half is payable to the rector, and the other to the Ecclesiastical Commissioners, in whom the benefice is sequestrated. There is neither church, glebe-house, nor glebe. In the R. C. divisions the parish forms the head of a union or district, comprising the parishes of Carrune, Noughaval, and Kilcorney ; there are two chapels, one at Crughville, in this parish, and one in the village of Noughaval. There are two pay schools, in which are about 90 boys and 60 girls. The parochial church is in ruins, and there are the remains of two other old churches at Crunane and Glanculmkil ; the burial-ground of each is still used. St. Columb is said to have founded an abbey at Glanculmkil, which subsequently became the parish church ; the bed of the saint, formed of stones, is still preserved as a relic. Some brass coins have been dug up here. Near St. Columb's bed is one of the finest springs in the country, but the water possesses no medicinal properties.

CLARE (County of), a maritime county of the province of **MUNSTER,** bounded on the east and south by Lough Derg and the river Shannon, which successively separate it from the counties of Tipperary, Limerick, and Kerry ; on the west by the Atlantic Ocean, and on the north-west by Galway bay ; while on the north and north-east an imaginary boundary separates it from the county of Galway. It extends from 52° 30′ to 53° (N. Lat.), and from 8° 15′ to 9° 30′ (W. Lon.) ; and comprises, according to the Ordnance survey, 802,352 statute acres, of which 524,113 are cultivated land, 259,584 unimproved mountain and bog, and 18,655 are occupied by rivers and lakes. The population, in 1821, was 208,089 ; and in 1831, 258,262.

The inhabitants of this tract, in the time of Ptolemy, are designated by him *Gangani,* and represented as inhabiting also some of the southern parts of the present county of Galway : in the Irish language their appellation was *Siol Gangain,* and they are stated, both by Camden and Dr. Charles O'Conor, to have been descended from the *Concani* of Spain. The present county formed from a very early period a native principality, designated *Tuath-Mumhan,* or *Thomond,* signifying "North Munster;" and contained the six cantreds of Hy Lochlean, Corcumruadh, Ibh

Caisin, Hy Garman, Clan Cuilean, and Dal Gaes. In *Hy Lochlean,* or *Bhurrin,* the present barony of Burren, the O'Loghlins or O'Laghlins were chiefs ; in *Corcumruadh,* the modern Corcomroe, the O' Garbhs, although that portion is stated by Ware to have been occupied by the septs of O'Connor and O'Loghlin ; in *Ibh Caisin,* the present Ibrickane, the Cumhead-mor O'Briens, this being the hereditary patrimony of the O'Briens or O'Bricheans ; in *Hy Garman,* the modern Moyarta, the O'Briens Arta ; and in *Clan Cuilean,* the present Clonderlaw, the Mac Namaras ; *Dal Gaes* comprised the more extensive districts included in the baronies of Inchiquin, Bunratty, and Tulla, forming the entire eastern half of the present county, and was ruled by the O'Briens, who exercised a supreme authority over the whole, and who preserved their ascendancy here from the date of the earliest records to a late period. Few have more honourably distinguished themselves in the annals of their country than these chiefs and their brave Dalcassian followers, especially in the wars against the Danes, who long oppressed this country with their devastations, and formed permanent stations on the Shannon, at Limerick and Inniscattery. From these and from the entire district they were, however, finally expelled, early in the 11th century, by the well-directed efforts of the great Brien Boroihme, the head of this sept, and monarch of all Ireland, whose residence, and that of his immediate successors, was at Kinkora, near Killaloe. About the year 1290, the Anglo-Norman invaders penetrated into the very heart of Thomond, and in their progress inflicted the most barbarous cruelties, especially upon the family of O'Brien ; but they were compelled to make a precipitate retreat on the advance of Cathal, prince of Connaught. De Burgo, in the year 1200, also harrassed this province from Limerick ; and William de Braos received from King John extensive grants here, from which, however, he derived but little advantage. Donald O'Brien, amid the storms of war and rapine which laid waste the surrounding parts of Ireland, was solicitous for the security of his own territories, and, as the most effectual method, petitioned for, and obtained from Hen. III., a grant of the kingdom of Thomond, as it was called, to be held of the king during his minority, at a yearly rent of £100, and a fine of 1000 marks. Nevertheless, Edw. I., by letters patent dated Jan. 26th, 1275, granted the whole land of Thomond to Thomas de Clare, son of the Earl of Gloucester, who placed himself at the head of a formidable force to support his claim. The O'Briens protested loudly against the encroachments of this new colony of invaders, and in a contest which speedily ensued, the natives were defeated, and the chief of the O'Briens slain ; but with such fury was the war maintained by his two sons, that the new settlers were totally overthrown, with the loss of many of their bravest knights : De Clare and his father-in-law were compelled to surrender, after first taking shelter in the fastnesses of an inaccessible mountain ; and the O'Briens were acknowledged sovereigns of Thomond, and acquired various other advantages. De Clare afterwards attempted with some success, to profit by the internal dissensions of the native septs. He died in 1287, at Bunratty, seized, according to the English law, of the province of Thomond, which descended to his son and heir, Gilbert de Clare, and, on the death of the latter without issue, to his brother, Richard de Clare. The O'Briens being subdued by Piers Gaveston, the latter greatly extended his power in this province, where, in 1311, he defeated the Earl of Ulster, who had commenced hostilities against him. Shortly after, the English again received a defeat from the O'Briens, and Richard de Clare, who died in 1317, had no English successor in these territories. Of the settlements made by these leaders, the principal were Bunratty and Clare, long the chief towns of the district ; and the English colonists still maintained a separate political existence here ; for so late as 1445, we find the O'Briens making war upon those not yet expelled. All of them, however, were eventually put to the sword, driven out, or compelled to adopt the manners of the country ; the entire authority reverting to the ancient septs, among whom the Mac Mahons rose into some consideration. In the reign of Hen. VIII., Murchard or Murrough O'Brien was created Earl of Thomond for life, with remainder to his nephew Donogh, whose rights he had usurped, and who was at the same time elevated to the dignity of Baron Ibrakin. Murrough was also created Baron Inchiquin, with remainder to the heirs of his body, and from him the present Marquess of Thomond traces his decent. On the division of Connaught into six counties by Sir Henry Sidney, then lord-deputy, in 1565, Thomond, sometimes called O'Brien's country, was also made shire ground, and called Clare, after its chief town and its ancient Anglo-Norman possessors. In 1599 and 1600, Hugh O'Donell plundered and laid waste the whole county : Teg O'Brien entered into rebellion, but was shortly after slain. In accordance with its natural position, the county, on its first erection, was added to Connaught ; but subsequently, in 1602, it was re-annexed to Munster, on petition of the Earl of Thomond.

With the exception of three parishes in the diocese of Limerick, it is included in the dioceses of Killaloe and Kilfenora, the whole of the latter being comprised within its limits : it is wholly in the province of Cashel. For purposes of civil jurisdiction it is divided into the nine baronies of Bunratty, Burren, Clonderlaw, Corcomroe, Ibrickane, Inchiquin, Islands, Moyarta, and Tulla. It contains the borough and market-town of Ennis ; the sea-port and market-town of Kilrush ; the market and post-towns of Curofin and Ennistymon ; the post-towns of Newmarket-on-Fergus, Six-mile-Bridge, Scariff, Killaloe, Kildysert, Miltown-Malbay, Burren, Knock, Broadford, and Bunratty ; the town and port of Clare ; and the smaller towns of Kilkee and Liscanor, the latter of which has a small harbour. The election of the two members returned by this county to the Imperial parliament takes place at Ennis ; the constituency registered under the late act consists of 300 £50 free-holders, 271 £20 freeholders, 1888 £10 freeholders, and 12 £20 and 47 £10 leaseholders ; making a total of 2518. The number of electors that polled at the last general election was 686. It never had more than one parliamentary borough, that of Ennis, which sent two members to the Irish parliament, and still sends one to that of the United Kingdom. Clare is included in the Munster circuit : the assizes are held at Ennis, and the quarter sessions at Ennis, Six-mile-Bridge, Kilrush, Ennistymon, and Miltown-Malbay. The county gaol is at Ennis, and there are bridewells at Kilrush, Tulla, Six-mile-Bridge, and Ennistymon. The number of persons charged with criminal offences and committed to the county gaol, in 1835, was 733, and of civil bill commitments, 182. The local government is vested in a lieutenant, 12 deputy-lieutenants, and 102 other magistrates, with the usual county officers, including three coroners. The number of constabulary police stations is 54, having in the whole a force of 8 chief and 62 subordinate constables, and 235 men, with 8 horses, maintained equally by Grand Jury presentments and by Government.   The peace preservation police consists of 1 magistrate, 3 chief and 18 subordinate constables, and 82 men, the total expense of whose support amounted, in 1835, to £5340. 0. 2. Parties of the revenue police are stationed at Ennis and

Killaloe. At Ennis are situated the county house of industry, and the county infirmary and fever hospital, besides which there are eleven dispensaries, situated respectively at Curofin, Doonass, Ballyvaughan, Six-mile-Bridge, Carrigaholt, Kilrush, Ennistymon, Tomgrany, Kildysert, Newmarket, and Killaloe, all maintained by Grand Jury presentments and voluntary contributions in equal portions. The total amount of Grand Jury presentments, for 1835, was £44,290. 8. 11., of which £4568. 14. 7$1/4$., was for the public roads of the county at large ; £11,452. 9. 10. for the public roads, being the baronial charge ; £16,291. 18. 5$1/2$. for public buildings and charities, officers' salaries, &c. ; £6699. 18. 9$1/4$. for police ; and £5277. 7. 3. in repayment of loans advanced by Government. In military arrangements this county is included in the south-western district, and contains the three barrack stations of Clare Castle, Killaloe, and Kilrush, affording in the whole accommodation for 19 officers and 325 men ; and there are small parties stationed at the respective forts or batteries of Kilkerin, Scattery Island, Dunaha, and Kilcredane, erected during the continental war to protect the trade of Limerick, and each affording barrack accommodation to 16 artillerymen ; and also at Aughnish Point and Finvarra Point, on the southern shore of the bay of Galway.

The county possesses every diversity of surface, and great natural advantages, which require only the hand of improvement to heighten into beauty. Of the barony of Tulla, forming its entire eastern part, the northern portion is mountainous and moory, though capable of improvement ; and the eastern and southern portions are intersected by a range of lofty hills, and are studded with numerous demesnes in a high state of cultivation ; and there is a chain of lakes extending through this and the adjoining barony of Bunratty, which might easily be converted into a direct navigable line of communication between Broadford, Six-mile-Bridge, and the river Shannon. Bunratty barony, which includes the tract between this and the river Fergus, has in the north a large proportion of rocky ground, which is nevertheless tolerably productive, very luxuriant herbage springing up among the rocks, and affording pasturage for large flocks of sheep. The southern portion of this barony, adjoining the rivers Fergus and Shannon, contains some of the richest land in the county, both for tillage and pasturage ; the uplands of this district are also of a superior quality. Inchiquin barony, lying to the north-west of

14

Bunratty, has in its eastern part chiefly a level surface, with a calcareous, rocky, and light soil ; the western consists for the most part of moory hills, with some valleys of great fertility : the part adjoining the barony of Corcomroe is highly improvable, limestone being every where obtained. The barony of Islands, which joins Inchiquin on the south and Bunratty on the west, is chiefly composed on the western side of low moory mountain, but towards the east, approaching the town of Ennis and the river Fergus, it greatly improves, partaking of the same qualities of soil as Bunratty, and containing a portion of the corcasses. Between this last and the Shannon is the barony of Clonderlaw, very much encumbered with bog and moory mountain, but highly improvable, from the facility of obtaining lime and sea manure. The four remaining baronies stretch along the western coast. That of Moyarta constitutes the long peninsula between the Shannon and the Atlantic, forming the south-western extremity of the county, and terminating at Cape Lean or Loop Head, where there is a lighthouse : this also abounds with bog and moory hills, capable of great improvement. The southern part of Ibrickane, which lies north of Moyarta, is nearly all bog, and the northern is composed of a mixture of improvable moory hills and a clay soil. Corcomroe, the next maritime barony on the north, is of the same character as the last-mentioned lands, having a fertile clay soil on whinstone rock, here called cold stone, to distinguish it from limestone : the land about Kilfenora and Doolan is some of the richest in the county. Burren, forming the most northern extremity of the county, is very rocky, but produces a short sweet herbage excellently adapted for the sheep of middle size and short clothing wool, of which immense numbers are raised upon it, together with some store cattle. Besides the numerous picturesque islands in the Shannon and Fergus rivers, there are various small islets on the coast, in the bay of Galway, and in the great recess extending from Dunbeg to Liscanor, called Malbay, an iron-bound coast rendered exceedingly dangerous by the prevalence of westerly winds : the principal of these is Mutton Island, besides which there are Goat Island and Enniskerry Island, the three forming the group of the latter name. The coast at Moher presents a magnificent range of precipitous cliffs, varying from 600 to nearly 1000 feet in height above the sea at low water, on the summit of which a banqueting-house in the castellated style has been lately erected by Cornelius O'Brien,

Esq., for the use of the public. The lakes are very numerous, upwards of 100 having names : the majority are small, though some are of large extent, namely, Lough Graney, Lough O'Grady, Lough Tedane, and Lough Inchiquin ; the last is remarkable for its picturesque beauty and for its fine trout. Turloughs, called in other places Loghans, are frequent ; they are tracts of water either forced under ground from a higher level, or surface water mostly collected on low grounds, where it has no outlet, and remains until evaporated in summer : there is a very large one at Turloghmore, two near Kilfenora, and more in other places. Although the water usually remains on the surface for several months, yet on its subsiding, a fine grass springs up, that supports great numbers of cattle and sheep.

The climate is cool, humid, and occasionally subject to boisterous winds, but remarkably conducive to health ; frost or snow are seldom of long continuance. So powerful are the gales from the Atlantic, that trees upwards of fifty miles from the shore, if not sheltered, incline to the east. On the rocky parts of the coast these gales cause the sea, by its incessant attrition, to gain on the land, but where sand forms the barrier, the land is increasing. The soil of the mountainous district, extending from Doolan southward towards Loop Head, and thence along the Shannon to Kilrush, and even still further in the same direction, together with that of the mountains of Slieveboghta, which separate the county from Galway, is generally composed of moor or bog of different depths, from two inches to many feet, over a ferruginous or aluminous clay or sandstone rock, highly capable of improvement by the application of lime, which may be procured either by land carriage or by the Shannon. A large portion of the level districts is occupied by bogs, particularly in the baronies of Moyarta and Ibrickane, where there is a tract of this character extending from Kilrush towards Dunbeg about five miles in length and of nearly equal breadth. On the boundaries of the calcareous and schistose regions the soils gradually intermingle, and form some of the best land in the county, as at Lemenagh, Shally, Applevale, Riverstown, &c. A piece of ground of remarkable fertility also extends from Kilnoe to Tomgraney, for about a mile in breadth. But the best soil is that of the rich low grounds called corcasses, which extend along the rivers Shannon and Fergus, from a place called Paradise to Limerick, a distance of more than 20 miles, and are computed to contain upwards of 20,000 acres. They are of various breadth, indenting the adjacent country in a great diversity of form. From 18 to 20 crops have been taken successively from them without any application of manure : they are adapted to the fattening of the largest oxen, and furnish vast numbers of cattle to the merchants of Cork and Limerick for exportation. The part called Tradree, or Tradruihe, is proverbially rich. These corcasses are called black or blue, according to the nature of the substratum : the black is most valuable for tillage, as it does not retain the wet so long as the blue, which latter consists of a tenacious clay. The soil in the neighbourhood of Quinn Abbey is a light limestone, and there is a large tract of fine arable country where the parishes of Quinn, Clonlea, and Kilmurry-Negaul unite.

The arable parts of the county produce abundant crops of potatoes, oats, wheat, barley, flax, &c. A large portion of the tillage is executed with the spade, especially on the sides of the mountains and on rocky ground, partly owing to the unevenness of the surface and partly to the poverty of the cultivators. The system of cropping too often adopted is the impoverishing mode of first burning or manuring for potatoes, set two or three years successively ; then taking one crop of wheat, and lastly repeated crops of oats, until the soil is completely exhausted : but it is gradually giving place to a better system. Fallowing is practised to some little extent ; and many farms are cultivated on an improved system, one important part of which is an alternation of green crops. An improved system of spade husbandry (trenching or Scotch drilling) has been lately introduced, and if generally adopted would be productive of great advantages. Vast quantities of potatoes, usually boiled and sometimes mixed with bran, are used to feed cows and other cattle in winter. Beans were formerly sown to a great extent in the rich lands near the rivers Shannon and Fergus, but this practice has greatly declined. Red clover and rye-grass are the only artificial grasses generally sown. The corcasses yield six tons of hay per Irish acre, and even eight tons are sometimes obtained. Except near the town of Ennis, there is but a very small number of regular dairies, a few farmers and cottagers supplying the neighbouring villages with milk and butter. A considerable quantity of butter is sent to Limerick from Ennis, being chiefly the produce of the pastures near Clare and Barntick ; and it is also now made by the small farmers in most parts, and sent to Limerick for exportation to

London. The pastures of Clare are of sufficient variety for rearing and fattening stock of every kind. A totally opposite character is presented by the limestone crags of Burren, and the eastern part of the baronies of Corcomroe and Inchiquin, which are, with few exceptions, devoted to the pasturage of young cattle and sheep, though in some places so rugged that four acres would not support one of the latter. Intermixed with these rocks, however, are found lands of a good fattening quality, producing mutton of the finest flavour, arising from the sweetness of the herbage, though to a stranger it might appear that a sheep could scarcely exist upon them ; the parishes of Kilmoon and Killeiny contain some of the best fattening land in the county. Large tracts of these mountains are let by the bulk and not by the acre. The other baronies likewise present every variety, from the rich corcass to mountains producing scarcely any thing but heath and carex of various sorts, barely sufficient for keeping young cattle alive. The enclosed pastures are often of very inferior quality, from the ground having been exhausted with corn crops, and never laid down with grass seeds, but allowed to recover its native herbage ; a gradual improvement, however, is taking place, but the great defect consists in not properly clearing the ground. In the eastern and western extremities of the county the pasture land usually consists of reclaimed mountain or bog, having a coarse sour herbage, intermixed with carex, and capable of sustaining only a small number of young cattle. The herbage between Poulanishery and Carrigaholt is remarkable for producing good milk and butter ; and that of the sand hills opposite Liscanor bay, and along the shore from Miltown to Dunbeg, is also of a peculiar kind : these elevations consist entirely of sands blown in by the westerly winds, and accumulated into immense hills by the growth of various plants, of which the first, and now one of the most common, was perhaps sea reed or mat weed. Besides the home manures, some farmers apply (though not to a sufficient extent) limestone gravel, which is found in different parts ; limestone, now used very extensively ; marl, of which the bed of the Shannon produces inexhaustible quantities, and by the use of which astonishing improvements have been effected in the neighbourhood of Killaloe ; other species of marl of less fertilising powers, dug at Kilnoe, and between Feacle and Lough Graney, in the barony of Tulla ; near the coast, sea-sand and sea-weed, with which the potatoe ground is plentifully manured, and which is frequently brought up the Fergus by boats to Ennis, and thence into the country, a distance of four miles. Ashes, procured by burning the surface of the land, until lately formed a very large portion of the manure used here, but the use of them is now much condemned, especially for light soils. Great improvements have been made upon the old rude implements of agriculture ; the Scotch plough is generally used. In the rocky regions the only fences are, of necessity, stone walls, generally built without mortar : walls ten feet thick, made by clearing the land of stones, are not uncommon in these districts. The cattle are nearly all long-horned, generally well-shaped about the head, and tolerably fine in the limb, good milkers and thrifty. A few of the old native breed are still found, chiefly in mountainous situations : they are usually black or of a rusty brown, have black turned horns and large bodies, and are also good milkers and very hardy. The improved Leicester breed has been introduced to a great extent and of late years the short-horned Durham and Ayrshire cattle have been in request and are becoming general. Oxen are not often used in the labours of husbandry. The short and fine staple of the wool of the native sheep has been much deteriorated by the introduction of the Leicester breed, but the encouragement of the South Down may in a great measure restore it. The breed of swine has been highly improved, the small short-eared pig being now universal. The breed of horses has also undergone great improvement ; the horse fair of Spancel Hill is attended by dealers from all parts of Ireland. The chief markets for fat cattle are Cork and Limerick ; great numbers of heifers are sent to the fair of Ballinasloe. Formerly there were extensive orchards in this county, especially near Six-mile-Bridge, and a few still remain. Very fine cider is made from apples of various kinds, mixed in the press, and it is in such repute that it is generally bought for the consumption of private families, principally resident.

Few counties present a greater deficiency of wood, yet few afford more favourable situations for the growth of timber where sheltered from the cold winds of the Atlantic : the practice of planting, however, is gaining ground, but the general surface of the county is still comparatively bare. The most valuable timber is that found in the bogs ; it consists of fir, oak, and yew, but chiefly the two former : in red bogs, fir is generally found ; in black bogs, oak. The fir is frequently of very large dimensions, and most of the farmers' houses near places where it can be procured are roofed with it. The manner of finding these trees is somewhat curious : very early in the morning, before the dew evaporates, a man takes with him to the bog a long, slender, sharp spear, and as the dew never lies on the part over the trees, he can ascertain their situation and length, and thrusting down his spear, can easily discover whether they are sound or decayed : if sound, he marks with a spade the spot where they lie, and at his leisure proceeds to extricate them from their bed. Along the coast of Malbay, where not even a furze bush will now grow, large bog trees are frequently found. The extensive boggy wastes are susceptible of great improvement : the only part not containing large tracts of this kind is the barony of Burren, the inhabitants of the maritime parts of which bring turf in boats from the opposite coast of Connemara. On the other hand, a considerable quantity of turf is carried from Poulanishery to Limerick bay, a water carriage of upwards of forty miles, for the supply of which trade immense ricks are always ready on the shore ; and sometimes the boats return laden with limestone from Askeaton and Aughnish. Although large tracts formerly waste, including all the corcasses, have been gained from the Fergus and the Shannon, yet a large portion of the marshes on their banks still remains subject to the overflow of these rivers. The fuel chiefly used is turf, but a considerable quantity of coal is now consumed by respectable families.

The principal minerals are lead, iron, manganese, coal, slate, limestone, and various kinds of building stone. Very rich lead-ore has been found near Glendree, near Tulla, at Lemenagh, and at Glenvaan in the barony of Burren ; a vein of lead was discovered, in 1834, at Ballylicky, near Quinn, the ore of which is of superior quality and very productive ; it is shipped at Clare for Wales. There are strong indications of iron in many parts, especially near the western coast ; but it cannot be rendered available until a sufficient vein of coal shall have been found in its vicinity. Manganese occurs at Kilcredane Point near Carrigaholt Castle, near Newhall, on the edge of a bog near Ennistymon, and at the spa well of Fierd, on the sea shore near Cross, where it is formed by the water on the rocks. Coal has been found in many places, particularly near the coast of the Atlantic, but few efforts have been made to pursue the search with a view to work it. The best slates are those of Broadford and Killaloe, of which the former have long been celebrated, though the latter are superior, and both are nearly equal to the finest Welsh slates ; the Killaloe quarry is worked to a greater depth than those of Broadford. Near Ennistymon are raised thin flags, used for many miles around for covering houses, but requiring strong timbers to support them. The Ballagh slates are however preferred for roofing, as being thinner than most of the same kind. There is another quarry of nearly the same sort near Kilrush, one near Glenomera, and others in the western part of the county. At Money Point, on the Shannon, a few miles from Kilrush, are raised very fine flags, which are easily quarried in large masses. Limestone occupies all the central and northern parts of the county, in a vast tract bounded on the south by the Shannon, on the east by a line running parallel with the Ougarnee river to Scariff bay, on the north by the mountains in the north of Tulla and the confines of Galway, and on the west by Galway bay and a line including Kilfenora, Curofin, and Ennis, and meeting the Shannon at the mouth of the Fergus. The limestone rises above the surface in Burren and in the eastern parts of Corcomroe and Inchiquin, and in some places presents a smooth and unbroken plane of several square yards ; the calcareous hills extending in a chain from Curofin present a very curious aspect, being generally isolated, flat on the summit, and descending to the intervening valleys by successive ledges. Detached limestone rocks of considerable magnitude frequently occur in the grit soils ; and large blocks have been discovered in Liscanor bay, seven or eight miles from the limestone district : in a bank near the harbour of Liscanor, water-worn pebbles of limestone are found and burned. At Craggleith, near Ennis, a fine black marble, susceptible of a very high polish, is procured. The shores of Lough Graney, in the north-eastern extremity of the county, produce a sand chiefly composed of crystals, which is sought for by the country people for upwards of 20 miles around, and is used for scythe boards, which are much superior to those brought from England : sand of similar quality is likewise procured from Lough Coutra, in the same mountains. Copper pyrites occur in several parts of Burren. An unsuccessful attempt to raise copper ore was made at Glenvaan. In the time of James I., as appears from a manuscript in the Harleian collection, there was a silver mine adjacent to O'Loughlin's castle in Burren ; and an old interpolator of Nennius mentions that precious metals abounded here. Antimony, valuable ochres, clays for potteries, and beautiful fluor spar, have likewise been discovered in small quantities.

Linen, generally of coarse quality, is manufactured by the inhabitants in their own dwellings, but entirely for home consumption. A small quantity of coarse diaper for towels is also made, and generally sold at the fairs and markets, as is also canvas for sacks and bags ; but this trade is now very limited. Frieze is made, chiefly for home use ; and at Curofin and Ennistymon, coarse woollen stockings, the manufacture of the adjacent country, are sold every market day, but the trade has considerably declined ; they are not so fine as the stockings made in Connemara, but are much stronger. The only mills besides those for corn are a few tuck-mills scattered over the country. The river Ougarnee, from its copiousness and rapidity, is well adapted for supplying manufactories of any extent, and runs through a populous country. Though the numerous bays and creeks on the Shannon, from Loop Head to Kilrush, are excellently adapted for the fitting out and harbourage of fishing boats, yet the business is pursued with little spirit. The boats that are used are not considered safe to be rowed within five miles of the mouth of the Shannon, and from their small size, the fish caught is not more than sufficient for supplying the markets of Limerick, Kilrush, and Miltown, and the southern and western parts of the county ; the northern and eastern being chiefly supplied from Galway. In the herring season from 100 to 200 boats are fitted out in this river for the fishery, which, however, is very uncertain. It is thought that a productive turbot fishery might be carried on in the mouth of the river, but there are no vessels or tackling adapted for it : the boats are chiefly such as have been used from the remotest ages, being made of wicker-work, and formerly covered with horse or cow hides, but latterly with canvas ; they are generally about 30 feet long, and only three broad, and are well adapted to encounter the surf, above which they rise on every wave. Kilrush has some larger boats. In Liscanor bay a considerable quantity of small turbot is sometimes caught. Fine mullet and bass are sometimes caught at the mouths of the rivers, and many kinds of flat fish, together with mackarel and whiting, are taken in abundance in their respective seasons. Oysters are procured on many parts of the coast; those taken at Pouldoody on the coast of Burren, have long been in high repute for their fine flavour. The bed is of small extent, and the property of a private gentleman, and they are not publicly sold. Near Pouldoody is the great Burren oyster bed, called the Red Bank, where a large establishment is maintained, and from which a constant supply is furnished for the Dublin and other large markets. Oysters are also taken at Scattery island and on the shores of the Shannon, particularly at Querin and Poulanishery, where the beds are small but the oysters good, and almost the whole of their produce is sent to Limerick. Crabs and lobsters are caught in abundance on the shores of the bay of Galway, in every creek from Black-head to Ardfry ; and are procured in smaller quantities on the coast of the Atlantic, from Black-head to Loop-head. The salmon fishery of the Shannon is very considerable, and a few are taken in every river. Eels are abundant, and weirs for taking them are extremely numerous. The commerce of the county consists entirely in the exportation of agricultural produce, and the importation of various foreign articles for home consumption : of this trade Limerick is the centre, although Kilrush likewise participates in it. The only harbours between the mouth of the Shannon and Galway bay, an extent of upwards of 40 miles, are Dunmore, which is rendered dangerous by the rocks at its entrance, and Liscanor, which is capable of properly sheltering only fishing-boats. The fine river Fergus is made but little available for the purposes of commerce, the trade with Limerick being chiefly by an expensive land carriage. The only corn markets are those of Ennis, Clare, and Kilrush, which are very abundantly supplied, and much grain is purchased at them for the Limerick exporters ; corn is also shipped for Galway at Ballyvaughan and New Quay, on the north coast.

The most important river is the Shannon, which first touches the county on its eastern confines as part of Lough Derg, and thence sweeps round by Killaloe (where it forms the celebrated falls) to Limerick, from which city to the sea, a distance of 60 miles, it forms a magnificent estuary, nine miles wide at its mouth, where it opens into the Atlantic, and is diversified by many picturesque islands, bays, and promontories. This noble river, which washes no less than 97 British miles of its coast, is the great channel of the trade of the county, and besides its maritime advantages, affords a navigable access to all the central parts of the kingdom and to Dublin : the navigation, however, was incomplete until, through the exertions of the Board of Inland Navigation, the obstacles at Killaloe were avoided by the construction of an artificial line for some distance. The numerous bays and creeks on both its sides render it, in every wind, perfectly safe to the vessels navigating to Limerick, the quays of which place are accessible to ships of 400 tons' burden. Very important projected improvements of the navigation of this noble river, involving an enormous expenditure, are detailed in the account of the city of Limerick. The Fergus, a river of this county exclusively, has its source in the barony of Corcomroe, and running through the lakes of Inchiquin, Tedane, Dromore, Ballyally, and several others, and receiving the waters of various smaller streams, pursues a southern course to the town of Ennis, where it is augmented by the waters of the Clareen ; whence, flowing by Clare, it spreads below the latter place into a wide and beautiful estuary, studded with picturesque islands, and opening into that of the Shannon : from this river it is navigable up to Clare, a distance of eight miles, for vessels of nearly 500 tons' burden, and up to Ennis for small craft. Its banks in many places present a rich muddy strand, capable of being enclosed so as to form an important addition to the corcass lands : it receives many mountain streams, and after heavy rains rises so rapidly, that large tracts of low meadow are occasionally overflowed and the hay destroyed. From Lough Ferroig, situated on the top of the mountain of Slieveboghta, in the barony of Tulla, and on the confines of Galway, issues a stream which runs southward into the beautiful Lough Graney, and winding hence eastward collects the superflous waters of Annalow Lough and Lough O'Grady, and, about two miles below the latter, falls into Scarriff bay, a picturesque part of Lough Derg. The fine stream of Ougarnee rises near and flows through Lough Breedy, communicates with Lough Doon, receives the waters of Lough Clonlea, and, after forming of itself a small lake near Mountcashel, pursues its southerly course by Six-mile-Bridge, and falls into the Shannon near Bunratty castle, about nine miles below Limerick ; the tide flows nearly to Six-mile-Bridge. The other considerable streams are the Ardsallas, Blackwater, and Clareen, and the Ennistymon river : the smaller streams are almost innumerable, except in the barony of Burren, which is scantily supplied. Except the canal between Limerick and Killaloe, there is no artificial line of navigation, although it has been proposed to construct a canal from Poulanishery harbour, about twelve miles from Loop-head, across the peninsula to Dunbeg, and another from the Shannon,

24

at Scariff bay, through Lough Graney, to Galway bay. The roads are numerous and generally in good repair : the principal have been much improved within the last few years, and many hills have been lowered. Soon after the famine and distress of 1822, a new road was made near the coast between Liscanor, Miltown-Malbay, and Kilrush, and another between the last-named place and Ennis. The roads recently completed or now in progress, in aid of which grants have been made by the Board of Public Works, are, a direct road leading from the newly erected Wellesley bridge at Limerick to Cratloe, partly at the expense of the Marquess of Lansdowne ; a road from Knockbreda to the boundary of the county towards Loughrea, extending along the eastern side of Lough Graney, and proposed to be continued to Kiltannan, towards Tulla and Ennis ; and a road along the shore of Lough Derg, between Killaloe and Scariff. A road has also been lately made, at the expense of the county, from Scariff bay along the northern side of Lough O'Grady and the western side of Lough Graney, to the boundary of the county towards Gort, with a branch to the south towards O'Callaghan's mills. The bridges are generally good : a handsome new bridge has been lately built, under the superintendence of the Board of Public Works, over the Fergus at Ennis, and another of large dimensions and elegant structure is now in progress over the Inagh near Liscanor.

The remains of antiquity are numerous and diversified. There are cromlechs at Ballygannor, Lemenagh, Kilnaboy, Tullynaglashin, Mount Callan and Ballykishen : near the last-named are two smaller, and the remains of a cairn. Raths abound in every part, and many have been planted with fir trees. One occupies the spot near Killaloe, where formerly stood King Brien Boroihme's palace, or castle, called Kinkora. Pillar stones occur only in a few places : some may be seen on the road between Spancel Hill and Tulla. Of the ancient round towers, this county contains five, viz., those of Scattery Island, Drumcleeve, Dysert, Kilnaboy, and Inniscalthra, in Lough Derg. Near the cathedral of Killaloe is the oratory of St. Moluah, supposed to be one of the most ancient buildings in Ireland. Thirty religious houses were founded in this county, but at present there are remains only of those of Corcomroe, Ennis, Quinn, Inniscalthra, and Inniscattery. At Kilfenora several ancient crosses of great curiosity are to be seen ; a very remarkable one is fixed in a rock near the church of

Kilnaboy ; and near the church and round tower of Dysert a very curious one lies on the ground. The castles still existing entire or in ruins amount in number to 120, of which the family of Mac Namara, it is traditionally said, built 57. There are 25 in the barony of Bunratty, of which those of Bunratty and Knopoge are inhabited ; 13 in Burren, of which those of Castletown and Glaninagh are inhabited, and Newtown castle is a round fortress on a square base ; 8 in Clonderlaw, of which that of Donogrogue is inhabited ; 14 in Corcomroe, of which that of Smithstown is inhabited ; 6 in Ibrickane ; 22 in Inchiquin, of which those of Mahre and Dysert are inhabited : 3 in Islands ; 4 in Moyarta, of which that of Carrigaholt is inhabited ; and 25 in Tulla. Many of them are insignificant places, built by the proprietors in times of lawless turbulence ; others, small castellated houses erected by English settlers. Bunratty castle, however, is of considerable extent, and was once considered a place of great strength. The modern seats are described under the heads of the parishes in which they are respectively situated. The better class of farmers and graziers have generally comfortable dwelling-houses and convenient offices, with roofs of slate or flags. The poorer classes are usually badly lodged in houses built of stone without mortar, the walls of which are consequently pervious to the wind and rain. The cottages are always thatched, either with straw, sedges, rushes, heath, or potatoe stalks: a want of cleanliness is universally prevalent. Few cottages are without sallow trees, for kishes or baskets, which many of the labourers know how to make ; and almost all have small potatoe gardens. The Irish yet spoken in the remote parts of the county is chiefly a jargon of Irish with English intermixed, and is rapidly falling into disuse. Hurling matches are a favourite sport of the peasantry, and chairs, or meetings of both sexes at night in some public-house, constitute another source of amusement. Mineral waters are found in many places, and are chiefly chalybeate : that at Lisdounvarna has long been celebrated for its efficacy in visceral complaints ; at Scool and Kilkishen are others well known ; and two more are situated near Cloneen, about a mile north-west of Lemenagh Castle, and at Cassino, near Miltown-Malbay. Many holy wells, remarkable naturally only for the purity of their waters, exist in different parts, but are little regarded, except by the peasantry. The great falls in the Shannon, near Killaloe, are worthy of especial notice. The title of Earl of Thomond, derived from this county, was raised to a Marquesate in 1800, in favour of the family of O'Brien, which also derives from the extensive territory of Inchiquin the titles of Earl and Baron, and from the district of Burren also that of Baron. The title of Earl of Clare is borne by the family of Fitzgibbon.

CLARE, a town, in the parish of **CLARE-ABBEY**, barony of **ISLANDS**, county of **CLARE**, and province of **MUNSTER**, 2 miles (S.) from Ennis ; containing 1021 inhabitants. It is situated on the river Fergus, about 12 miles from its confluence with the Shannon, is of great antiquity, and was formerly the capital of the county. In 1278 a great battle was fought here between Donell O'Brien and Mahon O'Brien, in which the latter was defeated. According to the annals of the Mac Brodies, the castle was built by Donogh O'Brien, surnamed Cairbreach, King of Thomond, and in 1641 was surprised and burnt by Murrough O'Brien, who took possession of the lands. Although the town contains some good slated houses, the greater number are thatched, and on the commons to the west, poor cottiers from various parts have located themselves and erected wretched cabins, which gives to this suburb an air of extreme poverty. On the site of the castle are cavalry barracks, affording accommodation for 17 officers and 234 men ; and, from its central situation, the town is well adapted for a military depot. Fairs are held on May 21st, Aug. 17th, and Nov. 11th. A great quantity of salmon is taken in the Fergus, and occasionally sold at the low price of 3*d*. per lb. The parochial church, a Roman Catholic chapel, the parochial school, and a dispensary, are in the town. This is one of the principal ports of the county for the export of grain, by means of the Fergus. The entrance to the river lies between Rinana Point, on the east, and Innismurry on the west, and is about 5 miles wide, but the ship channel does not exceed three-fourths of a mile in width, and is not adapted for vessels drawing more than 16 feet of water. The quay, although only 80 feet long, and therefore accommodating but one vessel at a time, is yet of considerable service, as before its erection in 1815 there were no means of shipping or discharging a cargo, and vessels of any kind very rarely visited the town. At present, one or two come every month, bringing coal and taking back grain to Liverpool, where, in 1831, it was sold at a higher rate than any other grain in the market. About 600 feet above the quay there is a bridge, the abutments of which rest on a solid bed of rock, forming an obstruction that separates the Upper from the Lower Fergus ; this bridge leads to an island, on which stand the remains of the castle. A second and smaller bridge, leading to the mail coach road to Limerick, crosses the arm of the river that runs round Castle Island. The main branch of the river, from the bridge to the quay, is about 250 feet wide. From Clare to Ennis by the Upper Fergus is three miles : this is a fine piece of water, about 150 feet wide, wearing much the appearance of a large canal. It sometimes overflows its banks, and greatly fertilises the adjacent country. To form a communication between the Upper and Lower Fergus, it is proposed to place a dam and lock at the falls, about a furlong above the bridge, and to deepen the bed of the river between those places from three to six feet, and between the quay and the bridge about four feet.

CLARE-ABBEY, a parish, in the barony of **ISLANDS**, county of **CLARE**, and province of **MUNSTER**, 2 miles (S.) from Ennis ; containing, with the town and commons of Clare, 3881 inhabitants. This parish is situated on the river Fergus, and on the road from Ennis to Limerick, and was the seat of a richly endowed abbey, founded in 1195, for Augustinian friars, by Donald O'Brien, King of Limerick. At the suppression, in 1543, it was granted to the Barons of Ibrackan by Hen. VIII., and in 1620 was given in fee to Donough, Earl of Thomond, which grant was confirmed, in 1661, to Henry, Earl of Thomond. The parish contains 6694 statute acres ; there are about 200 acres of bog, and the rest is principally in pasture ; sea-weed is procured for manure on the shores of the Fergus, and limestone exists in abundance. Two fairs are held annually at Clare ; and a seneschal's court for the recovery of small debts is held there monthly for the manor of Clonroad. The principal seats are Buncraggy, finely situated on the banks of the Fergus, and surrounded by a richly wooded demesne, the property of the Marquess of Conyngham, but now occupied by J. James, Esq. ; Carnelly, the seat of the representatives of the late Col. Stamer ; and Barntick, of D. Roche, Esq. The living is an impropriate cure, in the diocese of Killaloe, and in the patronage of the Bishop ; the rectory is impropriate in the Earl of Egremont, the representatives of Giles Daxon, Esq., and the Rev. F. Blood. Of the 6694 acres, the tithes of 1153, amounting to £35. 1. 6., are paid to the incumbent alone ; of 1005, amounting to £27. 13. 10., to the impropriators alone ; and of 1904, amounting to £54. 2. 9., in equal shares to the incumbent and impropriators : the remaining 2632 acres being unprofitable land, pay no tithes. The church is a neat structure with a square tower, erected in 1813, by aid of a gift of £800 from the late Board of First Fruits, and repaired recently by a grant of £162. 4. 7. from the Ecclesiastical Commisssioners. The glebe-house was built in 1822, by aid of a gift of £450 and a loan of £50 from the former Board. The glebe comprises 15 acres, subject to a rent of 10s. per acre, as £450 was paid by the late Board of First Fruits to reduce the rent. In the R. C. divisions this parish is the head of a union or district, called Clare, comprising the parishes of Clare-Abbey and Killone, in each of which is a chapel ; that at Clare is a thatched building, which it is intended shortly to re-erect on a larger scale. There is a school under the care of the incumbent, in which are about 50 children ; and there are two hedge schools, containing about 80 ; also a school under the superintendence of the parish priest. The remains of the abbey consist of a tower in   tolerable preservation, surmounted by graduated battlements, and the ivy clad walls of the abbey church, which together form a very picturesque object when viewed from a distance.

CLONDAGAD, or **CLONDEGAD**, a parish, in the barony of **ISLANDS**, county of **CLARE**, and province of **MUNSTER**, 7 1/4 miles (S. S. W.) from Ennis ;   containing 4650 inhabitants. This parish is situated on the west bank of the river Fergus, and contains 16,436 statute acres, of which 4711 are good arable and pasture land, and 11,725 are improvable bog and mountain. The arable land is good, and produces excellent crops of grain, which, with butter, pork, &c., are sent to Limerick from a small rudely constructed quay at Ballycorig. Good building stone abounds. A seneschal's court is held occasionally at Ballycorig for the manor of Clonroad, in which small debts are recoverable. The living is a vicarage, in the diocese of Killaloe, forming, with part of the rectory, the corps of the prebend of Clondagad in the cathedral of Killaloe, and in the patronage of the Bishop ; the other portion of the rectory is impropriate in John Scott, Esq. The tithes amount to £415. 7. 8 1/2., of which £230. 15. 4 3/4. is payable to the impropriator, and £184. 12. 3 3/4. to the vicar. The glebe-house was erected in 1812, by a gift of £400 and a loan of £296 from the late Board of First Fruits : the glebe comprises 3*a*. 3*r*. 22*p*. The church is a small plain building with a square tower, and was erected on the site of a former one by aid of a gift of £600, in 1808, from the same Board. In the R. C. divisions the parish is the head of a union or district, comprising also the parish of Kilchrist, and containing two chapels ; that for Clondagad is at Launa. There are five private schools, in which about 420 children are educated. At Ballycorig are some remains of the castle of that name.

CLONEY, or **CLONIE**, a parish, in the barony of **BUNRATTY**, county of **CLARE**, and province of **MUNSTER**, 4$_{1/2}$ miles (E. by N.) from Ennis ; containing 3531 inhabitants. This parish is situated on the road from Ennis to Tulla, and contains about 7695 statute acres, which are mostly in tillage, and agriculture is improving : there are about 2260 acres of bog. At Ballylisky a lead mine was discovered in 1834, yielding ore of superior quality, which is shipped for Wales at Clare. Fairs for live stock are held at Spancel hill on Jan. 1st, May 3rd, June 24th, Aug. 20th, and Dec. 3rd. In Clonie, the demesne of Burton Bindon, Esq., are a small lake, and the ruins of the old church and castle of Clonie. The living is a vicarage, in the diocese of Killaloe, and is part of the union of Quinn : the rectory is partly appropriate to the prebend of Tullagh in the cathedral of St. Flannan, Killaloe, and partly constitutes a portion of the sinecure union of Ogashin. The tithes amount to £221. 10. 9$_{1/4}$., of which £92. 6. 13$_{/4}$. is payable to the rector, £106. 3. 1. to the vicar, and £23. 1. 6$_{1/2}$. to the prebendary of Tullagh. In the R. C. divisions the parish forms part of the union or district of Quinn, in which the parochial chapel is situated, and there is a chapel of ease in the demesne of Clonie. At Spancel Hill is a school under the patronage of A. Hogan, Esq. ; and in the parish are two hedge schools, in which are about 130 boys and 60 girls.

CLONIE.-See **CLONEY.**

CLONLARA.-See **KILTONANLEA.**

CLONLEA, or **CLONLEIGH**, a parish, in the barony of **TULLAGH**, county of **CLARE**, and province of **MUNSTER**, 4$_{1/2}$ miles (N.) from Six-mile-bridge ; containing 3105 inhabitants. It comprises, exclusively of a large quantity of mountain and bog, 5355 statute acres, as applotted under the tithe act : the surface is partly occupied by lakes. The land is mostly in tillage, and some improvements have been made in the system of agriculture, from the judicious example of D. Wilson, Esq., and T. Studdert, Esq., the former of whom has planted to the extent of nearly 50 Irish acres within a few years. Limestone is abundant, and is extensively used for manure, there being 60 limekilns within this district. Two fairs are held annually at Enagh, and three at Kilkishen. A new road is in progress from Tulla to Limerick, through Kilkishen and by the Glonagruss mountain. The principal seats are Belvoir, the residence of D. Wilson, Esq. ; Glenwood, of Basil Davoren, Esq. ; Mount Baley of H. Baley, Esq. ; and Sion Ville, the property of T. Studdert, Esq. The living is a rectory and vicarage, in the diocese of Killaloe ; the rectory, with those of Kifinaghty, Kilseily, Killurane, Killokennedy, Kinloe, Feacle, and the half rectory of Ogonilloe, constitutes the union of Omullod, in the patronage of the Earl of Egremont ; the vicarage is in the patronage of the Bishop, who has the plough-land of Clonlea as part of his mensal. The tithes amount to £171. 18. 11/2. The glebe-house was erected by aid of a gift of £450, and a loan of £100, in 1815, from the late Board of First Fruits. The glebe comprises 101/4 acres, subject to a rent of £3 late currency per acre. The church at Kilkishen is a small neat structure, with a square tower, built by a gift of £800, in 1811, from the late Board of First Fruits, and repaired in 1834, by a grant from the Ecclesiastical Commissioners. In the R. C. divisions the parish is the head of a union or district, called Kilkishen, comprising the parishes of Clonlea and Killuran : there are three chapels, situated respectively at Kilkishen, at Oatfield, and at Callaghan's Mills in the parish of Killuran. A new school-house has lately been erected at Belvoir, to which is attached a model farm ; the cost of the building was £190, of which £76 was paid by D. Wilson, Esq., and the remainder by the National Board. There are also five other schools in the parish, one of which at Kilkishen is under the patronage of the parish priest. At Scart is a chalybeate spring. On the south-west bank of Clonlea lake are the ruins of the old parish church and the burial-ground. The old ruin of Stackpoole, formerly the seat of a family of that name, is beautifully situated in this parish, overlooking the lakes of Pollagh and Mount Cashel;

it is now the property of the Earl of Limerick, on whom it confers the title of Baron of Foxford.

CLONLOGHAN, a parish, in the barony of **BUNRATTY**, county of **CLARE**, and province of **MUNSTER**, 5 miles (W. by S.) from Six-Mile-Bridge ; containing 763 inhabitants. This parish is situated on the river Shannon, and contains 2711 statute acres as applotted under the tithe act, which are mostly in pasture : it includes part of the rich corcasses on the banks of the Shannon. Knockhane is the residence of P. McMahon, Esq. The living is a rectory and vicarage in the diocese of Killaloe ; the rectory is part of the rectorial union of Tomfinlough ; the vicarage is part of the vicarial union of Kilfinaghty. The tithes amount to £105. In the R. C. divisions the parish forms part of the union or district of Newmarket.

CLONROAD.-See **ENNIS**.

CLONRUSH, a parish, in the barony of **LEITRIM**, county of **GALWAY,** and province of **CONNAUGHT,** situated on Lough Derg, 10$_{1/2}$ miles (S. by W.) from Portumna ; containing 3084 inhabitants. It comprises 11,201 statute acres, as applotted under the tithe act, and valued at £2890 per annum : a great part is annually flooded by the Shannon, and it contains a large tract of poor marsh land. Iron mines exist in the mountains, and Lough Derg furnishes means of communication with Limerick and Dublin. At Tintrim is the seat of J. Burke, Esq., on which is a chalybeate spring ; and beautifully situated on the banks of the Shannon is Meelick, the ancient seat of the Burke family, but now uninhabited. It is a vicarage, in the diocese of Killaloe, and is part of the union of Inniscalthra ; the rectory is appropriate to the economy fund of the cathedral of Killaloe : the tithes amount to £130, of which £70 is payable to the economy fund and £60 to the vicar. In the R. C. divisions it is the head of a union or district, comprising the parishes of Clonrush and Inniscalthra, in each of which is a chapel. There are two public schools, one at Furness and one at Dromane.

CLOUNEY, or **CLONEY**, a parish, in the barony of **CORCOMROE**, county of **CLARE**, and province of **MUNSTER,**

3 miles (E. by S.) from Ennistymon, on the road to Ennis ; containing 3371 inhabitants. This parish comprises 9741 statute acres, which are mostly in tillage ; the land is good and the system of agriculture gradually improving ; there is a considerable quantity of bog. It is in the diocese of Kilfenora ; the rectory is part of the union and corps of the deanery of Kilfenora, and the vicarage forms part of the union of Kiltoraght. The tithes amount to £160, of which two-thirds are payable to the rector and the remainder to the vicar. Divine service is performed in the glebe-house of Kiltoraght. In the R. C. divisions it forms part of the union or district of Ennistymon, and contains a chapel at Tierlahan, near Kilthomas, in which a school is held ; and there are also two private schools, in which altogether are about 250 children.

CONEY ISLAND, county of Clare.-See **INNISDADROM.**

CORCOMROE.-See **ABBEY.**

COSCORY, or **ENNIS-CORKER,** an island, in the parish of **KILDYSART,** barony of **CLONDERLAW,** county of **CLARE,** and province of **MUNSTER,** 1 mile (E. by S.) from Kildysart. This island, which is inhabited by one family only, is situated near the western shore of the river Fergus, at its junction with the Shannon, and contains about 165 statute acres of excellent land, which is mostly in pasture ; the portion under tillage is manured with sea-weed, and produces good crops of grain and potatoes.

CRUSHEEN, a village, in the parish of **INCHICRONANE,** barony of **BUNRATTY,** county of **CLARE,** and province of **MUNSTER,** about 6 1/2 miles (N. N. E.) from Ennis, on the road to Gort ; containing 57 houses and 316 inhabitants. Fairs are held on the lands of "Brodagh by Crusheen" on Jan. 17th, May 20th, Aug. 15th, and Nov. 19th, for general farming stock. It is a constabulary police station, and has a dispensary. Petty sessions once a fortnight, and the road sessions for the district, are held here ; also a seneschal's court occasionally for the manor of Bunratty, in which small debts are recoverable. The old R. C. chapel stands here, and a new one is now nearly completed : in the ancient burial-ground, Sir Theobald Butler, who framed the articles of the Treaty of Limerick, lies interred.-See **INCHICRONANE.**

CUROFIN, or **COROFIN**, a small market and post-town, in the parish of **KILNEBOY**, barony of **INCHIQUIN**, county of **CLARE**, and province of **MUNSTER**, 7 miles (N. N. W.) from Ennis, on the road to Kilfenora, and 118 miles (W. S. W.) from Dublin ; containing 900 inhabitants. This town is situated about three-quarters of a mile south-east of Inchiquin lake, and near the western extremity of Lough Tadane : these loughs are connected by a river flowing through them, which is here crossed by a stone bridge. It comprises about 140 houses, mostly thatched, and consists of one main street, commencing near the bridge, and a shorter one branching off, towards the east, at the end of which stands the church, and on the south side of it the R. C. chapel. Considerable quantities of yarn stockings, the manufacture of the surrounding country, were formerly brought to this place for sale, but the trade has long been on decline. Adjoining the bridge is Richmond, the residence of the Rev. S. Walsh, P. P. ; and about three-quarters of a mile west of the town, and near the shore of Inchiquin lake, is Riverstown, the old mansion of the Burton family, now converted into a chief constabulary police station. A boat race has lately been established on the lake of Inchiquin (which is remarkable for the beauty of its scenery and for its fine trout), and is likely to become annual. Lough Tadane is said to abound with roach and very large pike. A small market is held on Wednesday ; and there are two fairs, one on the day before Ascension-day, and one on Nov. 22nd. The market-house is an old building, supported by slanting buttresses, and is at present almost disused, the corn being chiefly sent to Ennis. Petty sessions are held on alternate Wednesdays ; and road sessions for the district are also held here. A seneschal's court for the manor of Inchiquin is occasionally held, in which small debts are recoverable. The church is a small neat edifice. The R. C. chapel is a spacious slated building, erected by subscription about ten years since. The parochial school is chiefly supported by the Rev. Mr. Blood and Edward Synge, Esq. Here is also a large school, under the patronage of the parish priest. Hugh McCurtin, the learned antiquary, grammarian, and poet, author of an Irish dictionary, died here about 1720, and was interred at Kilvedane, in the neighbourhood.-See **KILNEBOY.**

CURRANROE, a village, in the parish of **ABBEY**, barony of **BURREN**, county of **CLARE**, and province of **MUNSTER**, 2 miles (E.) from Burren ; containing 92 inhabitants. This village is situated at the extremity of an inlet from the bay of Galway, which forms the harbour of Burren, or New Quay, into which the sea rushes with considerable force for nearly four miles, and up to Curranroe bridge, which forms the boundary of the counties of Clare and Galway. It is a neat and improving place, several slated houses having been erected within the last few years ; and is a station of the constabulary police. Here is a small quay, at which turf and sea manure are landed ; but in consequence of the new road lately made towards the interior, it is about to be removed, and a more commodious one constructed by Burton Bindon, Esq., who employs a considerable number of labourers in clearing the ground of stones, and placing them on the slab in the bay, to promote the growth of sea weed, in which a great trade is here carried on. Curranroe, the neat cottage residence and farming establishment of Mr. Bindon, is in the village, and in the vicinity is the great oyster bed called the Red Bank, which is described in the article on the parish of Abbey.

DEER ISLAND, or **INNISMORE**, an island, in the parish of **KILCHRIST**, barony of **CLONDERLAW**, county of **CLARE**, and province of **MUNSTER**, 3 1/2 miles (N. E.) from Kildysart ; the population is returned with the parish. This island is situated near the western bank of the river Fergus, about a quarter of a mile from the shore of Kildysart parish, and contains 493 statute acres, which are nearly equally divided between pasture and tillage. It is the property of the Earl of Egremont, and is also called Inchmore, or the "Great Island," being the largest of those by which the Fergus is adorned, and is remarkable for the fertility of its soil. Flax was formerly cultivated here to a considerable extent, and afforded employment to the female population, but it is now only partially grown. There are some vestiges of an abbey still remaining, founded (according to Archdall) at a very early period, by St. Senan of Inniscattery, who appointed St. Liberius, one of his disciples, to preside over it.

DONAMONA, a parish, in the barony of **TULLAGH**, county of **CLARE**, and province of **MUNSTER**, contiguous to the town of Killaloe, in which parish it has merged. It is a rectory, in the diocese of Killaloe, entirely appropriate to the economy estate of the cathedral of St. Flannan : the tithes amount to £42. 4. 3.

DOOGH.-See KILKEE.

DOWRY, or **DOWRIE**, a parish, in the barony of **BUNRATTY**, county of **CLARE,** and province of **MUNSTER**, 11/4 mile (E.) from Ennis, on the road from Clare to Spancel hill ; containing 2099 inhabitants. It comprises 3684 statute acres, as applotted under the tithe act, and consists chiefly of arable and pasture land of second and third rate quality : there are about 800 acres of bog, and a considerable portion of limestone crag. Sea-weed and sand brought up the river Fergus are much used for manure. The seats are Moriesk, the finely wooded demesne of the Rt. Hon. Lord Fitzgerald and Vesci ; Well-Park, that of the Rt. Rev. Dr. McMahon, R. C. Bishop of Killaloe ; Castle Fergus, of W. Smith Blood, Esq., and Tuoreem, of W. O'Connell, Esq. The parish is in the diocese of Killaloe ; the rectory is part of the union of Ogashin, and the vicarage of that of Quinn : the tithes amount to £217. 11. 61/4., of which, £102. 9. 3. is payable to the rector, £92. 6. 13/4. to the vicar, and £23. 1. 61/2. to the prebendary of Tullagh. In the R. C. divisions it forms part of the union or district of Kilraghtis : the chapel is a small thatched building, but a new and very handsome structure is about to be erected on another site. A school supported by Mr. Howley having been lately discontinued, it is in contemplation to establish another on a more general plan.

DROMCLIFFE, or **OGORMUCK**, a parish, in the barony of **ISLANDS**, county of **CLARE**, and province of **MUNSTER**, on the river Fergus, and on the road from Limerick to Galway ; containing, with the assize, market, and post-town of Ennis, 14,083 inhabitants. This parish, including Inch, comprises 8387 statute acres, as applotted under the tithe act. The land varies greatly in quality. There are about 240 acres of craggy pasture that might be easily converted into good arable land. At Cragleigh is some very fine close-grained black marble. The gentlemen's seats are Stamer Park, the residence of M. Finucane,

Esq. ; Abbeyville, of T. Crowe, jun., Esq. ; Willow Bank, of E. J. Armstrong, Esq. ; Greenlawn, of T. Mahon, Esq. ; Hermitage, of W. Keane, Esq. ; Cahircalla, of C. Mahon, Esq. ; Beechpark, of R. Keane, Esq. ; Ashline Park, of R. Mahon, Esq. ; Cranaher, of B. Blood, Esq. ; Brookville, of J. Mahon, Esq. ; and Green Park, of the Rev. W. Adamson. The living is a vicarage, in the diocese of Killaloe, united in 1818, to those of Kilnemona, Kilraghtis, and Templemaly, forming the union of Dromcliffe, in the gift of the Bishop. The rectory is partly impropriate in R. Keane, Esq., and partly united, in 1803, to the rectories of Kilnemona and Kilmaly, in the patronage of the Marquess of Thomond. The tithes of the parish amount to £332. 6. 2$1/2$., of which, £101. 10. 9$1/2$. is payable to the impropriator, a similar sum to the rector, and the remaining £129. 4. 7$1/4$. to the vicar ; the tithes of the vicarial union are £285. 16. 10$3/4$. The glebe contains four acres near the old church, which is in ruins : the present church at Ennis consists of part of the ancient Franciscan abbey. The site of the old glebe-house has been added to the church-yard, where, during the prevalence of the cholera, no less than 340 bodies were buried in one pit. In the R. C. divisions the greater part of the parish forms the union or district of Ennis, where the chapel is situated : the western part, called Inch, is the head of the district of that name, which also includes the parish of Kilmaly. A new chapel is now being built at Inch, and there is a chapel in Kilmaly. The number of children educated in the public schools, exclusively of the college, is 650 ; and there are seven private schools. Near the old church are the remains of one of the ancient round towers, of which about 50 feet are still standing. At Inch is a strongly impregnated chalybeate spring which is occasionally resorted to.- See **ENNIS.**

DROMCREHY, or **DRUMCREELY**, a parish, in the barony of **BURREN**, county of **CLARE**, and province of **MUNSTER**, 6 miles (W.) from Burren, on the bay of Ballyvaughan, and on the road from Burren to Kilfenora ; containing 1758 inhabitants. It comprises 6186 statute acres, as applotted under the tithe act, of which a considerable portion is rocky mountain pasture, principally devoted to the grazing of sheep. The substratum is limestone, which in various places rises above the surface. Sea-weed, an abundance of which is procured in the bay, is the principal manure. The seats are Harbour Hill, the cottage residence of G. Mc Namara, Esq. : Sans Souci, of the Rev. J. Westropp ; Ballyallaben, of J. O' Brien, Esq. ; Mucknish, of J. S. Moran, Esq. ; and Newtown Castle, of C. O'Loghlen, Esq. In the little creek of Pouldoody is a small oyster bed, the property of J. S. Moran, Esq., of Mucknish ; the oysters taken there have long been celebrated for their delicious flavour, and are always disposed of by the proprietor in presents to his friends. The living is a rectory and vicarage, in the diocese of Kilfenora, united, in 1795, to the rectories and vicarages of Glaninagh, Rathbourney, and Killonoghan, together constituting the union of Dromcreehy and corps of the treasurership of Kilfenora, in the patronage of the Bishop. The tithes of the parish amount to £115, and of the entire benefice, to £330. The church is in ruins ; that of the union is in the adjoining parish of Rathbourney. In the R. C. divisions the parish is part of the union or district of Glenarragha, or Glynn. A school is aided by the Duke of Buckingham, and another is about to be established. In this parish are the ruins of the castles of Mucknish and Ballynacraggy, and some vestiges of that of Ballyvaughan : at Newtown is a castle of unusual form, consisting of a round tower resting on a square base, and said to have been formerly the residence of the Prince of Burren ; it is in good preservation and inhabited. On the lands called "The Bishop's Quarter" are the remains of a religious house, of which no particulars are recorded.-See **BALLYVAUGHAN.**

DROMLINE, a parish, in the barony of **BUNRATTY**, county of **CLARE**, and province of **MUNSTER,** 3 miles (S. E.) from Newmarket, on the river Shannon, and on the mail coach road from Limerick to Ennis ; containing 1182 inhabitants. It comprises 2365 statute acres, as applotted under the tithe act, and contains a portion of the rich corcass lands on the banks of the Shannon, and about 370 acres of the Bishop's mensal lands. The land is partly in pasture, but chiefly in tillage, and the system of agriculture has been much improved. It is a vicarage, in the diocese of Killaloe, and forms the corps of the treasurership of the cathedral of Killaloe, and part of the union of Kilnasoolagh, in the gift of the bishop : the rectory is part of the sinecure union of Tradree, or Tomfinlogh, in the patronage of the Earl of Egremont. The tithes amount to £93. 8. 7$1/4$., of which £55. 7. 8$1/4$. is payable to the rector, and the remainder to the vicar. In the R. C. divisions this parish forms a portion of the union or district of

Newmarket : the chapel for this part of the district is a large building of modern date, situated near Ballycunneen. At Smithstown are the remains of an old castle, of which no particulars are recorded.

DUNBEG, or **DOONBEG,** a village, in the parish of **KILLARD,** barony of **IBRICKANE,** county of **CLARE,** and province of **MUNSTER,** 6 miles (N. W.) from Kilrush, on the bay of Dunmore; containing 213 inhabitants. The river Dunbeg flows into the harbour and is here crossed by a good bridge, near which stand the ruins of a lofty castle, formerly a defence to the harbour, and one of the ancient strong holds of the O'Briens. The harbour which is the only one, excepting Liscanor, between Loop head and the bay of Galway, an extent of nearly 40 miles, is rendered dangerous by the rocks at its entrance. The pier, built by the late Fishery Board, is small and not much frequented ; seaweed is landed here, and flags of a superior quality, raised near the village, are sent to Galway, Limerick, and Cork ; it also forms a place of refuge for small craft in bad weather. Here is a station of the coast-guard. Fairs are held on May 2nd, July 26th, Oct. 8th, and Dec. 16th, for general farming stock, and for flannel and frieze of home manufacture. Near the bridge is a flour-mill. A court for the manor of Kilrush, in which small debts are recoverable, is held once in six weeks. In the village is a R. C. chapel, and about a quarter of a mile from it is the newly erected parochial church.

DYNISH, county of CLARE.--See **INNISMACNAUGHTEN.**

DYSERT, or **DYSART,** a parish, in the barony of **INCHIQUIN,** county of **CLARE,** and province of **MUNSTER,** 4 1/2 miles (N. W.) from Ennis, on the road to Corofin ; containing 7279 inhabitants. This parish was formerly called Dysert O'Dea, from its having been the territory of the sept of that name. It comprehends the subdivisions of Inagh and Ruan, and contains 23,417 statute acres, as rated for the county cess, of which a large portion consists of coarse mountain pasture. There are about 300 plantation acres of common, 100 acres of wood, and 100 acres of bog. The waste land consists chiefly of crag and underwood, and several hundred acres are covered with water, there being a number of lakes that in winter overflow the adjoining land to a considerable extent. Limestone abounds, and is burnt for manure; and the state of agriculture is gradually improving. The river Fergus runs through the greater part of the parish, through Tedane and other lakes, to Clare Town. Fairs are held at Ruan on June 17th and Sept. 26th, the latter being one of the principal sheep fairs in the county. At Dysert and Ruan are stations of the constabulary police. A court for the manor of Inchiquin is occasionally held by the seneschal, for the recovery of small debts. The gentlemen's seats are Toonagh, the residence of C. O'Brien, Esq. ; Tierna, of Hewitt Bridgeman, Esq. ; Port, of H. O'Loghlen, Esq., Carhue, of E. Synge, Esq. ; Fountain, of E. Powell, Esq. ; Rockview, of R. O'Loghlen, Esq. ; Cogia, of T. Lingard, Esq. ; and Drumore, the property of R. Crowe, Esq. The parish is in the diocese of Killaloe : the rectory forms part of the union and corps of the prebend of Rath, and the vicarage, part of the union of Kilneboy. The tithes amount to £250. 13. 9., of which £165. 1. 2³/₄. is payable to the rector, £83. 17. 11. to the vicar, and £1. 14. 7¹/₄. to the prebendary of Tomgraney. There is a glebe of one plantation acre. In the R. C. divisions its northern and middle portions form the union or district of Dysert ; and the south-western portion (Inagh) gives name to a district, which also includes the parish of Kilnemona. In the former district are the chapels of Dysert and Ruan, and in the latter, those of Inch and Kilnemona. The chapel at Ruan was rebuilt by subscription in 1834. About 660 children are educated in two public schools at Dysert and Ruan, and about 70 in a private school ; to that at Dysert, E. Synge, Esq., contributes £24 per annum. Of the ruins of the churches of Dysert, Ruan, and Kiltala, the first is distinguished by its antiquity, and by the richly sculptured Saxon arch forming the doorway. Near these ruins are the remains of an ancient round tower, of which 30 feet are still standing ; about 20 feet from the ground is a doorway, and 10 feet higher are the remains of another ; at each stage the dimensions of the tower diminish, and outside the second story is a projecting belting-course. An ancient cross lies on the ground, bearing the effigy of a bishop, supposed to represent St. Monalagh, and other figures. A short distance from the ruins of Dysert church are those of the castle of that name, formerly the residence of the O'Deas ; and at Mahre, Ballygriffy, and Port, are the ruins of similar castles : those of Port, standing on the verge of a lake, have a picturesque appearance. In a house in this parish, the ruins of which can scarcely be traced, the old song to the air of "Carolan's receipt for drinking whiskey" is said to have been composed by three poets, of whom a ridiculous story is related concering the manner of writing it. For an account of the ancient sepulchral monument on Mount Callan, which extends into this parish, see **KILFARBOY.**

ENNIS, a borough, and market-town, in the parish of **DROMCLIFFE,** barony of **ISLANDS,** county of **CLARE,** (of which it is the chief town), and province of **MUNSTER,** 18 miles (N. W.) from Limerick, on the main road to Galway, and 111$3/4$ (S. W.) from Dublin ; containing 7711, and within the new electoral boundary, 9747 inhabitants. This place derives its name, formerly spelt Innis or Inish, signifying an island, from the insulation of a considerable plot of ground by the river Fergus. According to the Ulster Annals, it was anciently called *Inniscluan-ruadha*, and one of its suburbs is still called Clonroad. Mac Curtin states that it was eminent as a seat of learning, upwards of 600 scholars and 350 monks having been here supported by O'Brien, prince of Thomond, after the arrival of the English. About the year 1240, Donough Carbarac O'Brien erected a noble monastery at Ennis for Franciscan friars, which in 1305, according to the Annals of Innisfallen, was rebuilt or repaired and much adorned by another branch of that family. It was for a long period the place of sepulture of the princes of Thomond, and occasionally of the chiefs of the sept of Mac Namara ; and its prosperity appears to have been in these times dependent on this circumstance. In 1306, Dermot, grandson of Brien-Roe, at the head of a body of native and English forces, entirely destroyed the town. In 1311, Donogh, King of Thomond, bestowed the whole revenue of his principality for the enlargement and support of this monastery, and some time after the refectory and sacristy were built by Mathew Mac Namara. It is recorded in the Ulster Annals that Terence O'Brien, bishop of Killaloe, was here barbarously slain, in 1460, by Brien O'Brien. The friary was reformed by Franciscans of the Strict Observance : it remained in the Crown for some time subsequent to the Reformation, and was granted, in 1621, to Wm. Dongan, Esq. In 1609, Donogh, or Donat, Earl of Thomond, obtained a grant of a market and fairs to be held here ; and in 1612 "the town of Inish," was created a borough. In 1661, the goods of some of the towns people were seized in payment of salary due to Isaac Granier, one of their representatives in parliament, but were released on their stating, that he had agreed to serve gratuitously as their representatives.

It is situated nearly in the centre of the county, on the principal or south-western branch of the river Fergus, which surrounds a portion of the town and its north-eastern suburbs ; two of the principal streets form a continuous line following the winding of the river, and a third branches off from the court-house towards Limerick. The most populous of these is very narrow and irregularly built, and the entrance from Limerick is rendered equally inconvenient by a projecting angle of the court-house, which, from its dilapidated state, requires to be rebuilt. In 1831 the town comprised 1104 houses, and within the new electoral boundary, 1390 ; the suburbs, which are very extensive, consist chiefly of cabins. A new street of superior houses has been lately built between the county infirmary and the river ; and a handsome bridge of a single arch, with parapets of hewn stone, has been recently completed, at an expense of £800, on the site of a former one nearly opposite the abbey. The town is not lighted, and the police perform the duty of a nightly patrol. A county club-house has been established ; there are also two subscription news-rooms ; and races are held annually in the autumn, which generally continue five days. The numerous seats in the vicinity are noticed under the head of Drumcliffe and the adjacent parishes, in which they are situated. The woollen manufacture, which formerly flourished here, has greatly declined ; but the trade in corn, butter, and other produce has much increased. About 60,000 barrels of wheat, 100,000 of oats, and 30,000 of barley, are annually sold in the market, and chiefly shipped at Clare, about two miles distant, to which place the Fergus is navigable for lighters, and thence to the sea for vessels of considerable burden. A plan for improving the navigation between Ennis and Clare, is noticed in the account of the latter town, which is considered the port of Ennis. A weighing-house for butter, of which a large quantity is annually exported, was built in 1825, and there are several large corn stores. Ennis Mills, which have been recently enlarged, are capable of producing 30,000 barrels of flour annually : the produce is much esteemed in the Limerick market. At Clonroad is the extensive brewery of Messrs. Harley and Co., who are also about to re-establish a distillery formerly carried on at that place ; and there is a smaller brewery in the town ; the Ennis ale is in great repute. Branches of the Provincial and Agricultural Banks, and a savings' bank, have been established. A market for the sale of country produce is held daily, but the principal markets are on Tuesday and Saturday, and are abundantly supplied with provisions of every description. Fairs are held in the town on April 9th, and Sept. 3rd, and at Clonroad on May 9th, Aug. 1st, Oct. 14th, and Dec. 3rd ; of the latter, the first three are large fairs for cattle and horses, and the last is chiefly for pigs.

By the charter of the 10th of Jas. I. (1612), the corporation, under the style of "The Provost, Free Burgesses, and Commonalty of the Town of Ennis," consists of a provost, twelve free burgesses, and a town-clerk, with power to admit an unlimited number of freeman to constitute a "commonalty ; " but no freemen have been appointed for many years. The provost is elected by the burgesses from their own body, on the 24th of June, and sworn into office on the 29th of Sept. : until lately he appointed a deputy, called the vice-provost. The burgesses are elected for life by the provost and burgesses, who also appoint the town-clerk. The provost is empowered by the charter to hold a court of record, with congnizance of debts not exceeding £3. 6. 8. late currency, arising within the limits of the borough : this court was held until within the last 12 years, by the vice-provost, who also acted as weigh-master. By the charter the provost is a magistrate within the old borough, and the vice-provost formerly acted as such ; but latterly no exclusive jurisdiction, either civil or criminal, has been exercised. The borough sent two members to the Irish parliament prior to the Union, since which period it has returned one to the Imperial parliament : the right of election, formerly limited to the provost and free burgesses, was, by the act of the 2nd of Wm. IV., cap. 88, extended to the £10 householders ; and a new boundary was formed for electoral purposes, comprising an area of 469 statute acres, and comprehending the entire town and suburbs, which is minutely described in the Appendix. The number of voters registered, in March 1836, was 254, of which 7 were free burgesses, and the remainder £10 householders ; and the number polled at the last election was 194 : the provost is the returning officer. The spring and summer assizes, and the January, April, and October quarter sessions for the eastern division of the county, are held in the court-house. Petty sessions are held every Friday ; and a court for the manor of Clonroad, which was granted by Jas. I. to the Earl of Thomond, and now belongs to the Earl of Egremont, is occasionally held by the seneschal, for the recovery of debts not exceeding £10 late currency. The county gaol, situated on the south side of the town, is an extensive modern building on the radiating principle, with detached prisons for females and debtors, lately erected in front : it contains 10 day-rooms and airing-yards, 73 sleeping cells, and 12 other bed-rooms, and has a treadmil. The total expense of the establishment, for 1835, was £2522. 7. 10. The constabulary police force, including an extra force called the peace preservation police, is under the control of a resident stipendiary chief magistrate and a sub-inspector ; the barrack is a commodious building, formed out of the old county gaol. A party of the revenue police is also stationed in the town.

The parish church, which forms part of the ancient abbey, was much injured by lightning in 1817 ; the abbey tower was also damaged and the bell destroyed. The late Board of First Fruits granted £2000 for its renovation, and the tower was subsequently heightened by the addition of battlements and pinnacles : a grant of £146 has been recently made by the Ecclesiastical Commissioners for the further improvement of the church. The organ was presented, in 1825, by the Earl of Egremont. The R. C. district of Ennis comprises the eastern part of the parish of Dromcliffe, including the whole of the town and suburbs : the R. C. chapel is an old building, situated in an obscure part of the town. A chaste and elegant cruciform structure, from a design by Mr. Madden, was commenced in 1831, on a more eligible site, under the superintendence of the Very Rev. Dean O'Shaughnessy, P. P., which is intended for the cathedral of the R. C. diocese of Killaloe : the tower will be surmounted by a spire rising to the height of 140 feet. The estimated expense is £5000, towards which Sir Edward O'Brien, Bart., of Dromoland, contributed £100 : the site was presented by Francis Gore, Esq. A small society of Franciscans has a chapel which is open to the public ; and to the east of the town is an Ursuline convent, established about seven years since. There are meeting-houses for Primitive Methodists and Independents ; and a congregation of Separatists meet in the court-house : the Methodist meeting-house is a modern building, erected chiefly at the expense of Mr. Leach. Ennis college is one of the four classical schools founded by the munificent bequest of Erasmus Smith. The school-house,

44

which is situated at a short distance north of the town, was built about 70 years since by the trustees, who have recently added wings and out-offices, and made other extensive improvements, at an expense of nearly £1200 : it is now capable of accommodating more than 100 boarders, and a large number of day scholars. The building, which presents an imposing front, is approached from the extremity of the promenade called the "College walk" by a handsome gateway of four octangular pillars, and, together with the extensive play-ground, is surrounded by a high wall. The head master receives a salary of £100 from the trustees, and is allowed the full benefit of the establishment as a boarding and day school ; the second master also receives £100 ; and the third, £80. The course of instruction comprises the ancient and modern languages, mathematics, and English composition, and there are usually ten free day scholars on the foundation. The parochial school, in Jail-street, is supported by subscription ; a school is held in Cook's-lane meeting-house, and a Sunday school in the church. Near the town is a large and substantial school-house, built in 1830, at an expense of £800, of which £200 was contributed by the National Board, by whom the school, in which are about 400 boys, is partly supported, and partly by collections at the R. C. chapel. About 200 girls are instructed by the nuns of the convent, by whom they are also taught every description of useful and ornamental needlework. Connected with the nunnery-school is a preparatory establishment for very young girls, under the patronage of Dean O'Shaughnessy, who contributes £6 per ann. towards its support. The County Infirmary, situated on the north side of the town, is a substantial building, containing four wards for male and two for female patients, with a dispensary, and accommodations for a resident surgeon and apothecary. The Fever Hospital is situated in a confined part of the town, but one for the county is now been erected in a more appropriate situation and on a larger scale, to which a cholera hospital will be attached. The House of Industry immediately adjoins the infirmary, and contains three male and four female wards ; it was built by subscription about the year 1775, and is governed by a corporation under an act of the Irish parliament. A loan fund, for the benefit of the poorer classes of tradesmen and farmers, has been for some time in operation, and a mendicity society was established in 1832. The remains of the Franciscan abbey, founded by the Kings of Thomond, of whom several where interred in it, still present many traces of its ancient grandeur. Of these, the principal is the grand eastern window, upwards of 30 feet high, consisting of five lancet-shaped compartments, separated by stone mullions, and universally admired for its exceedingly light proportions and beautiful workmanship. In the chancel is the "Abbot's chair," which, with the altar, is richly sculptured with figures in high relief ; and some of the ancient monuments, also profusely sculptured, still exist.-See **DROMCLIFFE**.

ENNISKERRY, or **MUTTON ISLAND**, in the parish of **KILMURRY**, barony of **IBRICKANE**, county of **CLARE**, and province of **MUNSTER**, 1/2 a mile from the shore, on the western coast : the population is returned with the parish. It lies off that part of the coast which, from its rocky and dangerous character, is called the Malbay ; and contains about 210 statute acres of excellent land for feeding oxen and sheep, particularly the latter ; hence the name "Mutton island," from the fine flavour of the mutton. On its shores are some curious natural caves, formerly used by smugglers for storing contraband goods. Here are an old signal tower and the ruins of an ancient structure, said to have been an abbey, founded at a very early period by St. Senan of Inniscattery : the ancient name of the island was Inniscaorach.

ENNISTUBRET.-See **KILDYSART,** county of CLARE.

ENNISTYMON, a market and post-town, in the parish of **KILMANAHEEN**, barony of **CORCOMROE**, county of **CLARE,** and province of **MUNSTER**, 161/2 miles (W. by N.) from Ennis, and 128 (W. by S.) from Dublin, on the river Inagh, and on the mail road from Ennis to Miltown-Malbay ; containing 241 houses and 1430 inhabitants. The town, though irregularly built, has a picturesque appearance. A little below the bridge the river, which has its source in the mountains to the south-east, rushes over an extensive ridge of rocks and forms a beautiful cascade, at a short distance from which it joins the river Derry : the latter forms a junction with the river Inagh, and the united streams fall into the Altantic at Liscanor bay, about 21/2 miles west of the town. Races are occasionally held at Lahinch, on the bay of Liscanor, for the amusement of visiters during the bathing season. This place had formerly a considerable market for strong knit woollen stockings, which were purchased in large quantities by dealers for supplying Dublin and the north of Ireland ; but since the improvement in the stocking machinery this trade has gradually declined, and is now chiefly confined to the immediate neighbourhood. The market, which is held on Saturday, is well supplied with provisions, and is also a good mart for the sale of corn and pigs ; and fairs are held on March 25th, May 15th, July 2nd, Aug. 22nd, Sept. 29th, Nov. 19th, and Dec. 17th, for general farming stock. Sea-sand for manure is brought up the river, and in the vicinity are raised thin flags, used for roofing and other purposes : a body of manganese appears on the edge of a bog near the river. Coal was found in the neighbourhood several years since, and some of it sent to Galway and Limerick, but from its inferior quality the works were discontinued. Quarter sessions are held here four times in the year ; also petty sessions weekly on Monday. The sessions-house and district bridewell form a neat and commodious building, considered one of the best in the county. A seneschals' court for the manor of Ennistymon is held about once in each month, for the recovery of small debts. Here is a chief constabulary police station. The church, erected in 1830, is a handsome cruciform sturcture, in the later English style, with an octagonal tower on its south side resting on a square base : it is advantageously situated at the northern entrance of the town ; and on an eminence to the east are the ruins of the old church. The R. C. chapel is a large and substantial building, erected about 12 years since ; the old chapel has been converted into a school. The male and female free schools are supported by subscriptions, and by the proceeds of an annual charity sermon at the chapel ; a school is also supported partly by Archdeacon Whitty, and partly by the pupils' fees; and there is a public dispensary. Immediately adjoining the town is Ennistymon Castle, formerly a seat of the O'Brien family, descendants of the Earls of Thomond, and now the residence of Andrew Finucane, Esq. ; it is boldly situated on the north bank of the river, is surrounded by a richly wooded park, and contains some fine old family pictures. At a short distance is the glebe-house, the residence of the Ven. Archdeacon Whitty, a handsome and substantial mansion of recent erection, situated in a pleasing demesne, which is ornamented by young and thriving plantations. An abbey is said to have formerly

existed here, over which St. Luchtighern presided.-See
KILMANAHEEN.

FEACLE, a parish, in the barony of **TULLA**, county of **CLARE**,
and province of **MUNSTER**, 4 1/2 miles (W. N. W.) from Scariff,
on the new road to Gort ; containing 8844 inhabitants. This
parish, which is the largest in the county, comprises about 30,000
statute acres, of which two-fifths consist of arable and pasture
land, and the remainder, with the exception of 300 acres of
woodland, is coarse mountain pasture, waste, and bog, a large
portion of which is improvable. It presents, throughout, a
succession of mountain and valley, extending to the confines of
the county of Limerick, and includes the extensive and
picturesque lake called Lough Graney, or "the lake of the sun,"
situated nearly in its centre. Prior to the year 1828 there was
scarcely a road on which a wheel carriage could be used ; but
through the spirited exertions of Jas. Moloney, Esq., of Kiltannan,
excellent roads have been constructed, partly by the Board of
Public Works and partly by the county; and this district has now
a direct communication with Limerick, Gort, Ennis, Killaloe, and
Loughrea. These roads encompass three sides of Lough Graney,
the banks of which are in several places finely planted : the soil in
the vicinity of the lake is well adapted for the growth of oak and
larch ; and it is expected that planting will be extensively carried
on, and a considerable portion of the waste land brought into
cultivation. A beautiful river flows from this lake, which is 18
feet above the level of the Shannon, through Lough O'Grady, at
the south-eastern extremity and partly within the limits of the
parish, and falls into the Shannon at Scariff bay, with which a
navigable communication could be formed at a moderate
expense, by a canal about five miles in length. A court for the
manor of Doonas is occasionally held by the seneschal, in which
small debts are recoverable ; and it is in contemplation to
establish a court of petty sessions and a dispensary in the parish.
There are several tuck-mills and a large bleach-green ; and there
were formerly extensive iron-works at a place still called Furnace-
town. The gentlemen's seats are Caher, the occasional residence
of Barry O'Hara, Esq., situated in a finely planted demesne on the
banks of Lough Graney ; Ayle, the ancient seat of J. McNamara,
Esq. ; Lakeview, of T. Bridgeman, Esq. ; and Kilbarron, of E.
McGrath, Esq., rebuilt on the site of the old mansion. It is a

rectory, vicarage, and perpetual cure, in the diocese of Killaloe; the rectory is part of the union of Omullod, the vicarage, part of the economy estate of the cathedral of Killaloe, and the perpetual cure is in the patronage of the Dean and Chapter, who, as trustees of the economy fund, allot a stipend of £69. 5. to the curate. The church, a small neat edifice, was built about the year 1823, by aid of a gift of £300 from the late Board of First Fruits. The R. C. parish is co-extensive with that of the Established Church, and contains four chapels : the principal chapel, at Feacle, is a spacious cruciform structure, built in 1827, under the superintendence of the Rev. T. McInerny, at an expense of £1300 ; it is provided with galleries, and has a very handsome altar embellished with well-executed paintings and a very large bell : the site was granted gratuitously by Henry Butler, of Castle Crinn, Esq., who has also contributed £50 towards its erection. A school-house on an extensive scale is now being built near the chapel by subscription. The chapel at Killenana is intended to be rebuilt, and those at Kilcleran and Cahirmurphy to be taken down, and a large chapel erected at Knockbeagh, on a site presented by J. Molony, Esq., who will also contribute liberally towards its erection. In a school, superintended and partly supported by the R. C. clergyman, and four private schools, about 360 children are educated. Lead ore has been discovered at Glendree, and on the shores of Lough Graney is found a fine sand, chiefly composed of crystals, and much used for scythe boards.

FERMOYLE, or **LETTERCANNON**, a village, in the parish of **KILLONOGHAN**, barony of **BURREN**, county of **CLARE**, and province of **MUNSTER** ; containing 42 houses and 220 inhabitants.

FINOGH, or **PHINAGH**, a parish, in the barony of **BUNRATTY**, county of **CLARE**, and province of **MUNSTER**, 1 1/2 mile (N. W.) from Six-mile-bridge, on the road to Ennis ; containing 1021 inhabitants, and comprising 2632 statute acres, as applotted under the tithe act. The land is in general of good quality, and chiefly under tillage, and the state of agriculture is gradually improving. Fairs are held at Rossmanaher on Jan. 6th, May 10th, June 15th, Sept. 12th, and Oct. 16th, mostly for sheep and pigs. Immediately adjoining is Rossmanagher, the seat of Lieut.-Col.

Wm. O'Brien. The other seats are Deer Park, that of E. Mansell, Esq. ; Springfield, of F. Morice, Esq. ; and Streamstown, of E. Wilson, Esq. The parish is in the diocese of Killaloe ; the rectory forms part of the union of Tomfinlough, and the vicarage, part of the union of Kilfinaghty. The tithes amount to £150, of which two-thirds are payable to the rector, and the remainder to the vicar. In the R. C. divisions it is part of the union or district of Six-mile-bridge. About 30 children are educated in a school under the superintendence of the parish priest. The ruins of the old church still remain in the burial-ground, and at Rossmanagher are those of an ancient castle.

FINVARRA, a village, in the parish of **OUGHTMANNA**, barony of **BURREN**, county of **CLARE**, and province of **MUNSTER**, 21/2 miles (W.) from Burren, on the bay of Galway ; containing 410 inhabitants. This village, which is situated in a detached portion of the parish, is chiefly remarkable for a Point of that name which stretches into the bay from the peninsula formed by the parish of Abbey, and on which a martello tower has been erected. There is also a similar tower on Aughnish Point, to the north-east, which also forms a detached portion of the same parish. Finvarra Point is situated on the north-east side of the bay of Ballyvaughan, and to the south-west of the entrance of the harbour of New Quay.

FYNISH.-See **INNIS-MAC-NAUGHTEN.**

GLANINAGH, a parish, in the barony of **BURREN**, county of **CLARE**, and province of **MUNSTER**, 71/2 miles (W.) from Burren, on the southern shore of Galway bay ; containing 545 inhabitants, of which number, 220 are in the village. It comprises about 4200 statute acres, which chiefly consist of rocky mountain pasture ; the portion in tillage is manured with sea-weed, an abundance of which is procured in the bay. It comprehends the lofty headland called Blackhead, in lat. 53° 9' 20" and lon. 9° 13', along the north-eastern shore of which is deep water and shelter for large vessels. Several boats belonging to this parish are engaged in the fishery of Galway bay. A new line of road, about four miles in length, is now in progress along the coast round Blackhead, which will nearly complete the line of communication round the coast of the county. It is a rectory and vicarage, in the diocese of Kilfenora, forming part of the union and corps of the treasurership of the cathedral of Kilfenora : the tithes amount to £32. 10. In the R. C. divisions it is part of the union or district of Glyn, or Glenarraha. The ruins of the church still exist in the burial-ground.

HOG ISLAND.-See **KILRUSH.**

HOLY ISLAND-See **INNISCALTHRA.**

HORSE ISLAND, county of CLARE.-See **KILDYSART.**

INAGH, county of CLARE.-See **DYSERT.**

INCH, county of CLARE.-See **DRUMCLIFF.**

INCHICRONANE, or **INIS-CRONAN,** a parish, in the barony of **BUNRATTY**, county of **CLARE**, and province of **MUNSTER**, 5 1/2 miles (N. E.) from Ennis, on the road to Gort ; containing 4603 inhabitants. It is situated near the confines of the county of Galway, and comprises about 14,400 statute acres, of which one-fourth consists of mountain, and there are about 320 acres of bog. Within its limits are the lake and island of the same name, on which latter Donald O'Brien, King of Limerick, about the year 1190, founded an abbey for regular canons of the order of St. Augustine, which, with a portion of the tithes of this parish, was granted in 1620 to Donogh, Earl of Thomond, and, in the following year, again in fee to Henry, Earl of Thomond. The remains, situated at the western extremity of the island, are extremely interesting, and the scenery of the island and lake highly picturesque. The seats are Inchicronane, the beautiful demesne of the Rt. Hon. Lord Fitzgerald and Vesci ; Bunnahow, the residence of W. Butler, Esq. ; Milbrook, of Austin Butler, Esq.; and Glenwilliam, of J. B. Butler, Esq. It is a vicarage, in the diocese of Killaloe, forming part of the union of Kilneboy : the rectory is impropriate in the Rev. F. Blood and his heirs. The tithes, amounting to £134. 13. 11 1/2., are wholly payable to the incumbent, he being also the impropriator. Divine service is occasionally performed in a private house. In the R. C. divisions the parish forms a separate union or district, and contains the chapels of Crusheen and Meelick : a new chapel is now being erected at the former place. In a school under the superintendence of the R. C. clergyman, and in three other schools, about 410 children are educated. Besides the ruins of the abbey, there are some remains of the old parochial church, and of O'Brien's castle.- See **CRUSHEEN.**

INCHIQUIN, county of CLARE.-See **KILNEBOY.**

INISHERK.-See **KILDYSERT.**

INNISCALTHRA, INNISKELTAIR, or **HOLY ISLAND,** an island, in that part of the parish of **INNISCALTHRA,** which is in the barony of **TULLA,** county of **CLARE,** and province of **MUNSTER,** 4 miles (E.) from Scariff. This island, which is also called the "Island of the Seven Churches," is in Lough Derg, between the counties of Clare and Galway. St. Camin, who died about the middle of the seventh century, founded an abbey or church here, which was afterwards called Teampul Camin. In 834 the island was ravaged by the Danes from Limerick, and in 1027 the great Brien Boroimhe rebuilt the church. St. Camin, the founder of the abbey, is said to have written a commentary on the Psalms, which he collated with the Hebrew text. St. Coelan wrote a life of St. Bridget in Latin verse ; and Corcran, the most celebrated ecclesiastic of Western Europe for religion and learning, was abbot in the early part of the eleventh century. Here are the remains of seven small churches, which display considerable elegance of design. Here is also an ancient round tower in very good preservation, which is likewise called the Anchorite's Tower, from St. Cosgrath, an anchorite, having lived and died in it in the tenth century. This island is still a favourite burial-place, and is much visited by pilgrims. It contains about 25 acres of very rich land, and in its vicinity are Red Island and Bushy Island.

INNISCALTHRA, a parish, partly in the barony of **TULLA,** county of **CLARE,** and province of **MUNSTER,** but chiefly in that of **LEITRIM,** county of **GALWAY,** and province of **CONNAUGHT,** 4 miles (N. E.) from Scariff ; containing 2198 inhabitants. It takes its name from the celebrated island in Lough

Derg (above described), by which it is bounded on the south and east ; and comprises about 9000 statute acres, of which 2500 are arable, 4500 pasture, 1900 bog and waste, and 100 woodland. Much land has been reclaimed since 1820, and there is a large portion of the mountain land under pasture. Iron exists, which makes some of the springs chalybeate, and very fine limestone and sandstone are found at Sallarnane. The principal seats are Wood Park, the residence of P. Reade, Esq. ; and Kilrateera, of E. Reade, Esq. Petty sessions once a fortnight and fairs are held at Whitegates, in the vicinity. It is a vicarage, in the diocese of Killaloe, united in 1803 to the vicarages of Moynoe and Clonrush, and in the patronage of the Bishop ; the rectory is impropriate in the representatives of G. Tandy, Esq. The vicarial tithes amount to £23, and of the union to £119. 8. 5$_{1/2}$. There is a glebe-house, with a glebe of 12 acres in the parish of Clonrush. The church, in Mount-Shannon (*which see*), is a neat building, and was erected by aid of a loan of £390 from the late Board of First Fruits, in 1789, and repaired by a loan from the same Board in 1831. In the R. C. divisions it forms part of the union or district of Clonrush, and has a chapel at Mount-Shannon. There is also a meeting-house for Wesleyan Methodists, and a place of worship for Baptists. About 110 children are educated in a public and 20 in a private school. Near the shore is a circular Danish fort ; and silver coins of King John's reign, minted at Waterford, have been found in Wood Park bog.

INNISCATTERY, an island, locally situated off the shore of the parish of **KILRUSH**, barony of **MOYARTA**, county of **CLARE**, and province of **MUNSTER**, but considered to form a part of the parish of St. Mary, Limerick ; the population is returned with Kilrush. This island, which is situated near the mouth of the river Shannon, about two miles from the shore, was anciently called Inis-Cathay and Cathiana, and was one of the most celebrated places of religious resort during the earlier ages of Christianity in Ireland. A monastery was founded here in the sixth century, according to some writers by St. Senan, and according to others by St. Patrick, who placed it under the superintendence of that saint. Great numbers of monks are said to have come from Rome to this place, and to have placed themselves under the protection of St. Senan, who erected seven churches on the island for this community, which lived in such seclusion and austerity that no female was permitted to land on the island : the superiors have been styled indifferently abbots or bishops. In 538, St. Kieran is said to have left the island of Arran and to have become an inmate of this monastery, of which he was made Providore. St. Senan died in 544, and was buried in the abbey, where a monument was erected to his memory ; and in 580 St. Aidan was bishop of Inniscathay. The island was plundered in 816 by the Danes, who put many of the monks to the sword and defaced the monument of St. Senan ; and in 835 they again landed here and destroyed the monastery. Early in the 10th century, Flaithbeartach, abbot of this place, was elected King of Munster ; and in 950 the Danes had gained such ascendancy in this part of Ireland, as to make the island a permanent depot. In 975, many of these invaders having taken shelter here, were driven out with the loss of 500 of their number by Brien Boroimhe, King of Munster, and Domnhall, King of Jonnahainein. The island was again plundered by the Danes of Dublin, headed by Diarmuid Mac Maoilnamba, but they were overtaken and defeated by Donogh, son of Brien. In 1176 the abbey was plundered by the Danes of Limerick ; and three years afterwards, the whole island was laid waste by William Hoel, an English knight, who destroyed even the churches. Soon after the death of Aid O'Beachain, Bishop of Inniscathay, the diocese of which this island was the seat was either united to that of Limerick, or divided among those of Limerick, Killaloe, and Ardfert. The monastery, notwithstanding the calamities it had suffered, subsisted till the dissolution, and in 1583 was granted by Queen Elizabeth to the mayor and citizens of Limerick.

The island, which is held on lease under the corporation of Limerick by F. Keane, Esq., who has a neat lodge here, contains more than 100 acres of very good land, but the sea is making rapid encroachments upon it. In the western portion is found a fine blue marl ; about one-sixth part only is under tillage, and the remainder in pasture ; the land in the immediate vicinity of the churches is remarkably fertile. The Scattery roads, which lie off its eastern shore, afford secure anchorage for large vessels ; and at the southern extremity, opposite the north-western point of Carrigafoyle, on the Kerry side of the Shannon, is a battery mounting six 24-pounders, with a bomb-proof barrack for 20 men, which is defended by two howitzers. In the ecclesiastical arrangements, the island, with part of the rectory and vicarage of

Kilrush, and of the rectories of Kilfieragh, Moyarta, and Kilballyhone, constitutes the prebend of Inniscattery in the cathedral of Killaloe, and in the patronage of the Bishop, the gross revenue of which is £653. 7. 10₁/₄. Among the numerous relics of antiquity is an ancient round tower, by recent measurement 117 feet high, which, though split from the summit to the base by lightning, and having a considerable breach on the north, still stands erect, forming a venerable feature in the scene, and a very useful landmark in the navigation of the Shannon. There are also the remains of the seven churches, and of several cells of the ancient monastery ; in the keystone of the east window of the largest of the churches is a sculptured head of St. Senan ; to each of them was attached a cemetery, some of which are still used as burial-grounds. There are also some remains of a castle, near the ruins of the monastery and churches, all towards the north-east side of the island, and presenting a remarkably interesting and highly picturesque appearance. From the number of ancient cemeteries on the island, and its having been the scene of numerous battles, the soil contains vast numbers of fragments of human bones, which in some parts have subsided into a stratum several feet beneath the surface, and which the sea in its encroachments is constantly exposing to view. An ancient bell, covered with a strong coating of silver, and ornamented with figures in relief was found here, and is preserved by Mr. Keane ; it is said by O'Halloran to have belonged to St. Senan's altar, and is held in such veneration, that no person would venture to swear falsely upon it ; it is used for the discovery of petty thefts, and called "the golden bell." Here is also a holy well, to which multitudes formerly resorted on Easter-Monday ; and numerous legendary traditions are current among the peasantry of the surrounding districts, by whom the island is still held in great veneration. From some Latin verses in Colgan's life of St. Senan, the distinguished poet Moore has taken the subject of one of his melodies, commencing "Oh! haste and leave this sacred isle."

INNISDADROM, or **CONEY ISLAND,** a parish and island, in the barony of **ISLANDS,** county of **CLARE,** and province of **MUNSTER,** 3₁/₂ miles (N. E.) from Kildysart ; the population is returned with the parish of Clondagad. It is situated nearly in the centre of the river Fergus, about a mile and a quarter from its western shore, and is estimated to contain about 226 statute acres;

it is at present inhabited by about 10 families. The land is remarkably fertile, and chiefly in tillage ; the substratum of the soil is limestone, and there is an abundant supply of sea-manure. Between this island and a ridge of rock, called Rat island, is a sound through which vessels drawing 11 feet of water can pass with a leading wind; it is narrow, and not more than two fathoms deep at low water, but the tide passes through it rapidly. It is a rectory and vicarage, in the diocese of Killaloe, forming part of the union of Lateragh and of the corps of the precentorship in the cathedral of Killaloe ; but it is stated in the late report of the Ecclesiastical Commissioners that the parish is withheld from the precentor, although mentioned in his titles. The ruins of two ancient churches still remain, of which that situated at the eastern extremity of the island appears to have been the principal.

INNISKELTAIR.-See INNISCALTHRA.

INNISMACNAUGHTEN, an island, in the parish of **KILCONRY**, barony of **BUNRATTY**, county of **CLARE**, and province of **MUNSTER**, 4 miles (W.) from Bunratty; the population is returned with the parish. It is situated on the eastern shore of the river Fergus, near its junction with the Shannon, and comprises 260 statute acres of land of a superior quality for fattening cattle. To the north-west is the island of Dynish, containing 20, and westward is that of Fynish, containing 160, acres of a similar quality. The latter island was, according to Archdall, anciently called *Inis-fidhe*, or *Cluan-fidhe*, and was the seat of a nunnery over which St. Bridget presided in the fifth century : the ruins of the old church still exist. Near Fynish is the "Priest Rock," a rugged straggling mass dangerous to vessels, on which it has been recommended to place a beacon, or pillar.

INNISTYMON.-See ENNISTYMON.

KILBAHA, a village, in the parish of **KILBALLYHONE**, barony of **MOYARTA**, county of **CLARE**, and province of **MUNSTER**, 15 1/2 miles (S. W.) from Kilrush, on the northern shore of the estuary of the Shannon ; containing 77 houses and 460 inhabitants. It is situated on the small bay of the same name, which is the first on entering the Shannon, and forms an asylum harbour for fishing vessels and other small craft coming in from Loop Head. The pier, constructed by the late Fishery Board, affords accommodation for landing sea manure, of which a considerable quantity is used in the neighbourhood, and has proved of great benefit to the farmers. Turf of a superior quality is cut in the vicinity, and sent hence to Limerick ; and the fisheries afford exclusive employment to upwards of 100 persons.-See **KILBALLYHONE.**

KILBALLYHONE, or **KILBALLYOWEN**, a parish, in the barony of **MOYARTA**, county of **CLARE**, and province of **MUNSTER**, 13 miles (S. W.) from Kilrush, on the western coast ; containing 3695 inhabitants. This parish is situated at the south-western extremity of the county, and, being bounded on one side by the Atlantic Ocean and on the other by the river Shannon, forms a peninsula which terminates in the promontory called Cape Lean, or Loop Head. It also comprises the headlands of Dunmore and Kilclogher, and the harbour of Kilbaha on the Shannon ; and its north-western shore forms part of the Malbay coast, on which numerous shipwrecks have occurred. The peninsula is exposed to the whole ocean swell, which here sets in with great violence in west or southerly winds, particularly when accompanied by the "rollers," a periodical visitation. Loop Head is situated at the mouth of the Shannon, in lat. 52° 33' 13", and long. 9° 54'. On its summit is a lighthouse, the lantern of which is 269 feet above the sea at high water, and exhibits a brilliant fixed light from 15 lamps. The parish comprises 9524 statute acres, as applotted under the tithe act. The land is chiefly in tillage, but there is a considerable portion of coarse pasture, with some patches of bog. Sea-weed and sand are extensively used for manure, and the state of agriculture is gradually improving. Samphire of superior quality is found on the cliffs at Clehansevan. It is in the diocese of Killaloe : the rectory is partly impropriate in the representatives of Lord Castlecoote, and the remainder forms part of the corps of the prebend of Tomgraney, in the cathedral of Killaloe ; the vicarage is part of the union of Kilrush. The tithes amount to £267. 13. 10 1/4., of which £69. 4. 7 1/2. is payable to the lessees of the impropriator, £83. 1. 6 1/2. to the prebendary, and £115. 7. 8 1/4. to the vicar. In the R. C. divisions it forms part of the union or district of Donaha, or Cross, which also comprises the parish of Moyarta, and contains three chapels, situated respectively at Cross, Donaha, and Carrigaholt. The ruins of the old church still remain in the burial-ground, and at Ross are those of another, but much smaller. Of the ancient castle of Clehansevan, which was blown down by a violent storm in 1802, some vestiges still exist ; and at Fodera hill are the remains of a signal-tower. The puffing holes of Clehansevan are considered a great natural curiosity, and in a certain state of the wind and tide spout water to a considerable height. At such times the sea is strongly impelled into the horizontal fissures of the cliff, and the air forced inwards by the weight of water suddenly reacting on the spent force of the waves, repels them with a sound resembling the discharge of heavy artillery. The natural bridges at Ross are formed by the action of the tide on the loose earth among the rocks. At Fierd is a chalybeate spring ; and manganese, adapted for making bleaching liquid, is also said to exist there.

KILCHRIST, a parish, in the barony of **CLONDERLAW**, county of **CLARE,** and province of **MUNSTER**, 3 miles (N. N. E.) from **KILDYSART**, on the western bank of the river Fergus; containing, with the island of Innismore, or Deer Island, 2569 inhabitants. This parish comprises 6845 statute acres, as applotted under the tithe act, and mostly under tillage ; there is a small extent of bog. Sea-weed and sand procured on the shores of the Fergus are extensively used for manure. Grain and other agricultural produce are occasionally sent in boats to Limerick from Ballinacally. The principal seats are Paradise, the residence of Thos. Arthur, Esq., beautifully situated on the Fergus, of which and the surrounding scenery it commands a most extensive view; and Fort Fergus, of Daniel O'Grady, Esq. ; is also situated on the Fergus. On an eminence in the demesne of Paradise is an ornamental building, called the Temple, which forms a conspicuous landmark in the navigation of the river. The parish is in the diocese of Killaloe : the rectory is partly impropriate in the Earl of Egremont, and partly in Bindon Scott, Esq. ; and the vicarage forms part of the union of Kildysert. The tithes amount to £252. 13. 10$1/4$., of which £83. 1. 6$1/2$. is payable to the lessee of the Earl, £64. 3. 3$3/4$. to Bindon Scott, Esq., and the remainder to the vicar. In the R. C. divisions it forms part of the district of Clondegad: the chapel, at Knockboy, is a small thatched building. A school is held in it under the superintendence of the R. C.

clergyman, in which and in three private schools about 140 children are educated. The ruins of the ancient church still remain in the burial-ground.-See **BALLINACALLY** and **DEER ISLAND.**

KILCONRY, a parish, in the barony of **BUNRATTY,** county of **CLARE**, and province of **MUNSTER,** 3$_1$/$_2$ miles (W. by S.) from Bunratty ; containing 793 inhabitants. This parish is situated at the junction of the rivers Fergus and Shannon, by the former of which it is bounded on the west and by the latter on the south, and comprises 2709 statute acres, as applotted under the tithe act. It comprehends the three inhabited islands of Dynish, Fynish, and Innismacnaughten, which contain land of a superior quality for fattening cattle ; and the rich corcass lands on the banks of the Fergus and Shannon yield a succession of 14 or 15 crops without manure of any description. At Isle Ruagh is a small quay, where sea-weed and turf are landed, and whence corn is occasionally sent in boats to Limerick. The gentlemen's seats are Stonehall, the residence of Thos. McMahon, Esq., and Carrigeary, of Major Creagh, both comanding extensive views of the estuary of the two rivers. The parish is in the diocese of Killaloe; the rectory forms part of the rectorial union of Tomfinlough or Traddery, in the patronage of the Earl of Egremont ; and the vicarage is part of the vicarial union of Kilfinaghty, in the gift of the Bishop. The tithes amount to £105, two-thirds of which are payable to the rector and the remainder to the vicar. In the R. C. divisions it forms part of the union or district of Newmarket, which is held by the administrator of the R. C. bishop of Killaloe : the chapel is at Carrigeary. Near Stonehall is a small school.

KILCORNEY, a parish, in the barony of **BURREN**, county of **CLARE**, and province of **MUNSTER**, eight miles (N. N. E.) from Curofin, near the road from Kilfenora to Ballyvaughan ; containing 335 inhabitants. The living is a rectory and vicarage, in the diocese of Kilfenora, united from time immemorial to the rectories and vicarages of Kilheny and Oughtmanna, which together constitute the union of Kilcorney and corps of the chancellorship of Kilfenora, in the gift of the Bishop : the tithes amount to £20, and those of the union to £165. There is neither church nor glebe-house, but a glebe of 18$_1$/$_2$ acres. In the R. C.

divisions this parish forms part of the union or district of Carrune. About 65 children are educated in a school superintended by the R. C. clergyman. The ruins of the ancient church still remain in the burial-ground. Near the village is a remarkable cave, the mouth of which is level with the ground : from the interior of this cave, which is of considerable extent, water is occasionally spouted into the air to a great height, and inundates the plain, although it is at some distance from any river or lake, and nearly 6 miles from the sea.

KILDYSART, or **KILLADYSERT,** a post-town and parish, in the barony of **CLONDERLAW,** county of **CLARE**, and province of **MUNSTER,** 12 miles (S. S. W.) from Ennis, and 122 miles (S. W.) from Dublin, at the confluence of the rivers Shannon and Fergus, and on the old mail road from Ennis to Kilrush ; containing 4501 inhabitants, and comprising 9485 statute acres, as applotted under the tithe act, which are chiefly in tillage. Sea-weed and sand are in general use for manure, and the state of agriculture is gradually improving: there is a considerable portion of bog. Culm exsists in some places and is partially worked ; and good building stone, which is also used for flagging, is procured. Off the western shore of the Fergus, and within the limits of the parish, are the islands Canon (which is described under its own head), Corcory, Ennistubret, Innisherk, Low and Horse, all of which are inhabited by one or more families. Corcory contains 103 plantation acres of excellent land, mostly in pasture; Ennistubret, 80 acres of similar land ; Innisherk, 18 acres ; Low, 85 acres, and Horse, 85 acres ; the two last are chiefly in tillage. The town, which contains about 60 houses, is irregularly built, but has latterly been much improved : a steam-boat passes daily either to or from Limerick. It has a market on Wednesday under a patent, and it is in contemplation of Bindon Scott, Esq., to build a market-house. Fairs are held on May 22nd, July 15th, Aug. 27th and Oct. 11th. Petty sessions are held every alternate Monday; and a court for the manor of Crovreahan is held by Lord Egremont's seneschal, about once in 6 weeks, in which small debts are recoverable. Here is a chief station of the constabulary police, who have a substantial barrack. Application has been made to the Board of Public Works for aid in the erection of a pier at Carriginriree, and to improve the quay near Kildysart : from the latter, pigs, corn, butter, and other agricultural produce are sent to Limerick in boats ; and building materials, grocery, &c., are brought in return : vessels of 105 tons have been freighted at this quay. The gentleman's seats are Ballyartney, the residence of R. Barclay, Esq. ; Ross Hill, of Major Ross Lewin ; Shore Park, of D. O'Grady, Esq. ; Lanesborough, of T. R. Lewin, Esq. ; Crowhan, of J. O'Donnell, Esq. ; Ballylane Lodge, of W. Coppinger, Esq. ; and Tonlagee, of the Finucane family. Part of the beautifully situated demesne of Cahircon, the seat of Bindon Scott, Esq., also extends into this parish, from the more elevated parts of which extensive views are obtained of the rivers Fergus and Shannon, and of the numerous islands by which the former is studded at its confluence with the latter. The living is a vicarage, in the diocese of Killaloe, united to the vicarage of Kilchrist and the rectory of Kilfarboy, and constituting the union of Kildysart, in the patronage of the Earl of Egremont : the rectory is impropriate in Bindon Scott, Esq. The tithes amount to £415. 7. 8¼., of which £276. 18. 5. is payable to impropriator, and the remainder to the vicar. The church, a small plain building, was erected in 1812, for which the late Board of First Fruits gave £500 : it is at present in a dilapidated state, and is about to be repaired or rebuilt, the Ecclesiastical Commissioners having recently granted £122 for that purpose. The glebe-house is a substantial building, for the erection which the late Board of First Fruits gave £400 and lent £240 : the glebe comprises about 12 acres. In the R. C. divisions this parish gives name to a union or district, which also comprises the parish of Kilfedane and contains the chapels of Kildysart, Coulmeen (or Rockmount) and Cranny bridge : the first is a handsome and spacious building of recent erection, and contains a well-executed alter-piece : the other chapels are in the parish of Kilfedane. About 230 children are educated in two private schools ; and a public school has been lately erected in the town. The ruins of the old church still remain in the burial-ground near the shore, and there are many Danish forts and tumuli in the parish. A monastery is said to have been founded on Low Island by St. Senan of Inniscattery, before St. Patrick came into Munster ; and St. Moronoc is said to have had a cell here at the time of St. Senan's death called, "the Penitentiary of Inisluaidhe."

KILFARBOY, a parish, in the barony of **IBRICKANE**, county of **CLARE**, and province of **MUNSTER**, 5 miles (S. S. W.) from

Ennistymon, on the western coast ; containing, with the post-town of Miltown-Malbay, 6389 inhabitants. It was anciently called Kilfobrick, from the monastery of that name, founded in 741, of which Cormac, who died in 837, is said to have been bishop, but of which no traces now remain. In the reign of Elizabeth, part of the Spanish Armada was wrecked on this coast, at a place which has since been called "Spanish Point." The parish comprises 11,637 statute acres, as applotted under the tithe act, a considerable portion of which consists of mountain pasture and bog ; sea-weed, which abounds, is in general use for manure, but the state of agriculture is rather backward. Mount Callan, which forms a conspicuous land-mark, is chiefly in this parish : in one of its hollows is Loughnamina, noted for its fine trout. Indications of coal and ironstone appear in several places; slate is found at Freagh ; and at Bellard, near Miltown, stone of superior quality is quarried for building. At Freagh is a station of the coast-guard, having also a detachment at Liscannor. The gentlemen's seats are Miltown House, the residence of T. H. Morony, Esq. ; Merville Lodge, of J. Carroll, Esq. ; Seaview, of F. G. Morony, Esq. ; Westpark, of J. Morony, Esq. ; and Spanish Point, of J. Costello, Esq., M. D. : and there are several neat lodges in the vicinity of Miltown-Malbay (*which see*) for the accommodation of the numerous visiters who frequent that fashionable watering-place during the summer. The parish is in the diocese of Killaloe : the rectory forms part of the union of Kildysart ; and the vicarage was episcopally united, in 1801, to that of Kilmihill or Kilmichael, together constituting the union of Kilfarboy, in the gift of the Bishop. The tithes amount to £553. 16. 11., of which £315 is payable to the rector and the remainder to the vicar ; those of the vicarial union amount to £312. 13. 10. The church, at Miltown, is a small plain edifice with a square tower, built in 1802, towards which £500 was granted by the late Board of First Fruits : it is about to be repaired, the Ecclesiastical Commissioners having lately granted £104 for that purpose. The glebe-house was erected in 1813, for which a gift of £337 and a loan of £79 were granted by the late Board : the glebe comprises about eight acres. In the R. C. divisions this parish forms part of the union or district of Miltown, which also comprises the parish of Kilmurry-Ibrickane, and contains two chapels, situated respectively at Miltown and Mullogh : the former is about to be rebuilt on a larger scale. There are two public schools, one of which is partly supported by the parishioners, and the other by the R. C. clergyman, and in which about 140 children are educated ; there are also five private schools, in which are about 230 children. On the shores of this parish are several springs of a chalybeate nature, but not much used for medicinal purposes. At Freagh are the ruins of the castle of that name, and there are several ancient raths or forts. At the side of Loughnamina, on Mount Callan, a very large and remarkable sepulchral stone of great antiquity was discovered, about 1784 ; it bears an inscription, in the ancient Ogham character, having the peculiarity of being read in five different ways, to the memory of the chief Conan, whose death is alluded to in one of the legends of the 8th century (ascribed to Ossian), as having taken place the year before the battle of Gabhra, which was fought in 296. From the hard texture of the stone the inscription, when discovered, was perfectly legible. On the south side of the mountain is a large cromlech, or druidical altar, nearly perfect, supposed to have been dedicated to the sun, and popularly called Darby and Grane's Bed; and near it are two smaller ones, and the remains of a stone rath, in which part of a covered way is still visible.

KILFEDANE, a parish, in the barony of **CLONDERLAW**, county of **CLARE**, and province of **MUNSTER**, 4 1/2 miles (W. S. W.) from Kildysart, on the river Shannon, near its junction with the Fergus ; containing 4165 inhabitants. It comprises 8981 statute acres, as applotted under the tithe act, including a large tract of improvable mountain and bog : the portion in tillage is generally manured with sea-weed and sand. Culm is found at Shanahea and partially worked. Within the parish are the mansion and principal part of the demesne of Cahircon, the seat of Bindon Scott, Esq., beautifully situated at the confluence of the Fergus and Shannon, of which an eminence near the house commands an extensive and interesting view, embracing a large portion of the shores of those rivers and the numerous islands by which their estuary is studded. Adjoining the demesne is Clifton House, lately erected by Bindon Scott, and not yet tenanted ; it occupies a beautiful situation contiguous to the shores of the Shannon, of which it commands an extensive view. There is a ferry from Clifton to Foyne's Island, on the opposite shore of the Shannon. The parish is in the diocese of Killaloe : the rectory is impropriate in Bindon Scott, Esq., and the vicarage forms part of the union of

Kilmurry-Clonderlaw. The tithes amount to £267. 13. 10$1/4$., of which £166. 3. 1. is payable to the impropriator, and the remainder to the vicar. In the R. C. divisions it forms part of the union or district of Kildysart : the chapel at Coulmeen is a large building of recent erection ; and at Cranny bridge, on the border of the parish, is another. About 60 boys are educated in a school, partly free, under the superintendence of the R. C. clergyman ; and there are four private schools, in which are about 210 children. A school-house is about to be built at Coulmeen by subscription. There are some ruins of the old church. About 1780, when an East India fleet took refuge in the Shannon, an encampment was formed in the deer-park of Cahircon.

KILFENORA, a decayed market-town and parish, and the seat of a diocese, in the barony of **CORCOMOROE**, county of **CLARE**, and province of **MUNSTER**, 4$1/2$ (N. N. E.) from Ennistymon, on the road to Curofin ; containing 2752 inhabitants, of which number, 558 are in the town. This place, called anciently Fenabore and Cellumabrach, though evidently of great antiquity, has not been much noticed by the earlier historians ; the first mention that occurs of it is in the annals of Ulster, in which it is stated that Murrough O'Brien, in 1055, burnt the abbey, and slew many of the inhabitants. In the 12th Century, the religious establishment which had been founded here, though originally by whom or at what date is unknown, became the head of a small diocese. The town appears to have been formerly of some importance, and a market was held there, but since the increase of Ennistymon it has been gradually declining ; the market is no longer held, and it has dwindled into an inconsiderable village ; fairs are, however, still held on the 4th of June and 9th of October, for cattle and sheep.

The EPISCOPAL SEE is of very uncertain origin, neither is it precisely known who was the first bishop ; though many are of opinion that St. Fachnan, to whom the cathedral is dedicated, must have been the founder. Of his successors, who were called bishops of Corcomroe, there are but very imperfect accounts, and of the history of the see very little is preserved. In the ancient distribution of the bishopricks, made by Cardinal Paparo in 1152, this see was made suffragan to the Archbishop of Cashel. It remained a separate diocese till after the Restoration, when it was annexed to the archbishoprick of Tuam, and continued for 81 years to be held with that diocese, till, on the annexation of Ardagh to Tuam, it was separated from it and given in commendam to the bishoprick of Clonfert, with which it was held till 1752, when it was united to the see of Killaloe, with which it still remains. It is one of the twelve dioceses which constitute the archiepiscopal province of Cashel, and is the smallest in Ireland ; it lies wholly within the county of Clare, and comprehends only the baronies of Burrin and Corcomroe, which formed part of the ancient territory of Thomond. It extends 23 miles in length and 11 in breath, comprising an estimated superficies of 37,000 acres. The lands belonging to the see comprise 9237 acres, of which 2350 are profitable land ; the gross annual revenue of the bishoprick is returned with that of Killaloe. The chapter consists of a dean, presenter, treasurer, and archdeacon ; there are neither minor canons, prebendaries, nor vicars choral : a consistorial court is held occasionally by the vicar-general. It comprises 19 parishes, which are included in six unions ; there are three parish churches, and one other place in which divine service is performed, and three glebe-houses. The cathedral church, dedicated to St. Fachnan, and which is also used as the parish church, is a very ancient and venerable structure with a massive square tower, commanding a very extensive and interesting view ; the aisle is at present undergoing repair, and is being fitted up as the parish church, for which purpose the Ecclesiastical Commissioners have granted £421. In the R. C. divisions this diocese is united to that of Kilmacduagh, and comprises eight unions, in which are 15 chapels, served by eight parish priests and two coadjutors.

The parish comprises 9236 statute acres, as applotted under the tithe act, a considerable portion of which is good grazing land, and the remainder under profitable cultivation ; the system of agriculture is improving, and there is a large portion of valuable bog. To the east of the village is a large turlough, which in summer affords very rich pasture for fattening cattle, but in the winter is under deep water after heavy rains. A new road has lately been made between the town and Ennistymon, with great benefit to the intervening district. Ballykeale, a seat of the Lysaght family, now occupied by Mrs. Fitzgerald, and Holywell, the residence of T. F. Comyn, Esq., are within the parish. The living is a rectory and vicarage, in the diocese of Kilfenora, united from time immemorial to the rectories of Clouney and Kiltoraght, together constituting the corps of the deanery of Kilfenora, in the patronage of the Crown : the tithes amount to £250, and of the whole union to £416. 13. 4. In the church are two monuments, of which one is supposed to be that of the founder, bearing a full-length effigy rudely sculptured, and to the north of the transept is another. The Deanery, towards the erection of which the late Board of First Fruits contributed a gift of £300, and a loan of £450, was erected about the year 1813 ; and has been greatly improved by the present occupant, the Very Rev. W. H. Stackpoole, D. D., who has added an extensive range of out-offices to the house ; in the shrubberies is a perfect ancient rath thickly planted. The glebe and deanery lands comprise 231 plantation acres, of which 70 are good pasture and the remainder mountain land ; and the gross annual value of the deanery, tithe, and glebe inclusive, is £482. 18. In the R. C. divisions the parish is held with that of Kiltoraght ; the chapel is a neat modern edifice in the village, and a chapel is now in course of erection in the parish of Kiltoraght. About 200 children are taught in two public schools, of which one is supported by the Dean, who, in conjunction with Sir W. McMahon, is about to erect a school-house. At Kilcarragh, very near this place, on the estate of Sir W. McMahon, was anciently an hospital or monastery, endowed with a quarter of land, and which, after the dissolution, was granted to John King. Near the cathedral is a stone cross of very light and beautiful design ; and in the churchyard is a plain cross of great antiquity : there were formerly seven crosses around this place, but these are the only two remaining.

KILFENTINAN, a parish, in the barony of **BUNRATTY**, county of **CLARE**, and province of **MUNSTER**, contiguous to the post-town of Six-mile-Bridge (of which it includes a small portion) ; containing 2856 inhabitants and comprising about 3600 acres, as rated for the county cess. It is situated on the northern shore of the river Shannon, and comprehends the two small inhabited islands of Grass and Graigue, containing respectively six and five plantation acres of rich pasture land. Near the latter is a rocky shoal called "the Scarlets," on which is a low tower erected as a guide to the navigation of the river. On the shores of this parish are some of the rich corcasses, which yield a succession of abundant crops without any manure. The land is mostly in tillage, and the state of agriculture has been latterly improved. A court for the manor of Bunratty is occasionally held at Cratloe, by

Lord Egremont's seneschal, in which small debts are recoverable. Here is a station of the constabulary police. The seats are Cratloe Woods, the occasional residence of Stafford O'Brien, Esq. ; and Ballintlea, of J. Kelly, Esq. The living is a vicarage, in the diocese of Limerick, and in the patronage of the Earl of Egremont, in whom the rectory is impropriate : the tithes amount to £267. 10., of which £197. 10. is payable to the impropriator, and £70 to the vicar. The R. C. parish is co-extensive with that of the Established Church. The principal chapel is at Cratloe Cross, and there is another at Ballyliddane, near Six-mile-bridge. About 120 children are educated in four private schools, and application is about to be made to establish a school at Cratloe, under the National Board. The ruins of the castles of Cratloe, Cratloe Kail, and Ballintlea, still remain ; also of the old church on Gallows hill, and of another at Crochan. Near the latter is a very perfect druidical alter or cromlech.

KILFIERAGH, a parish, in the barony of **MOYARTA**, county of **CLARE**, and province of **MUNSTER**, 7 miles (W. by N.) from Kilrush, on the western coast ; containing 6239 inhabitants. It comprises of 8591 statute acres, the greater part of which is under tillage : sea-weed is in general use for manure. Near Kilkee is a quarry of good building stone, and nearly in the centre of the parish is Dough bog, containing about 200 plantation acres, from which and other bogs extending into the adjoining parishes a vast quantity of turf is cut, and sent from Poulanishery harbour (formed by an inlet of the river Shannon) to Limerick. The boats employed in conveying the turf return with building materials and with limestone from the Limerick side of the Shannon. At Farahie bay, near the northern extremity of the parish, about 50 canoes are employed in the fishery ; and at Kilkee, or Moore bay, about half that number are similarly employed. A seneschal's court is occasionally held at Lisdeen for the manor of Kilrush, in which small debts are recoverable. The seats are Atlantic Lodge, the residence of Jonas Studdert, Esq. ; and Kilkee, of J. McDonnell Esq. ; and there are several neat bathing lodges in the vicinity of Kilkee. The parish is in the diocese of Killaloe : the rectory is partly impropriate in the representatives of Lord Castlecoote, but chiefly, with the vicarage, forms part of the union of Kilrush and corps of the prebend of Inniscattery : the tithes amount to £287, of which £37 is payable to the impropriators, and the remainder to the incumbent. The church, a small plain building without a tower, is said to have been rebuilt by the McDonnell family early in the last century ; it was repaired a few years since, at an expense of £100, defrayed by the late Board of First Fruits. Applications have been made to the Ecclesiastical Commissioners for aid in the erection of a new parochial church at Kilkee, the present being too small, and situated at a considerable distance from the most populous part of the parish. In the R. C. divisions it forms part of the union or district of Kilkee, where the principal chapel, a large and handsome building of recent erection, is situated : there is another chapel at Lisdeen. At Kilnahallagh, on the western side of Poulanishery harbour, a nunnery is said to have been founded by St. Senan : it is called Kilnacaillech, or "the Church of the Nuns ;" and the ruins of the chapel still exist, with a burial-ground attached. Near Moore bay is a small rocky island, nearly inaccessible from the height of its cliffs ; it is traditionally stated that a bishop was at some former period here starved to death, and it is still called *Ilawn an uspug usthig*, or "the Island of the Starved Bishop." Near Kilkee is a large fort or rath, attributed to the Danes.-See **KILKEE**.

KILFINAGHTY, a parish, in the barony of **TULLA**, county of **CLARE**, and province of **MUNSTER**, on the river Ougarnee, and on the old road from Limerick to Ennis ; containing, with the greater part of the post-town of Six-mile-bridge, 4132 inhabitants. It comprises 7212 statute acres, including a large portion of coarse mountain pasture and bog ; the remainder is in general of good quality, and chiefly under tillage. Slate exists, but is not worked. The gentlemen's seats are Castle Crine, the residence of H. Butler, Esq. ; Mount Ivers, of W. Ivers, Esq. ; Castle Lake, of J. Gabbett, Esq. ; Springfield, of F. Morrice, Esq. ; and Mount Ivers Lodge, of E. Ferriter, Esq. It is in the diocese of Killaloe : the rectory forms part of the union of Omullod, and the vicarage is united to those of Kilmurrynegaul, Tomfinlough, Finogh, Clonloghan, Kilconry, and Bunratty, constituting the union of Kilfinaghty, in the gift of the Bishop. The tithes amount to £177. 15. 2 3/4., of which £85. 7. 4 3/4. is payable to the rector, and the remainder to the vicar, who receives the entire tithes of the townland of Ballysheenmore, containing 180 plantation acres; and the entire tithes of the vicarial union amount to £330. 9. 4. The church of the union is at Six-mile-bridge, and the glebe-house is in the parish of Bunratty. In the R. C. divisions it forms part of the union or district of Six-mile-bridge, where the chapel is situated. About 210 children are educated in three private schools. At Ballysheen are the ruins of an ancient church, with several tombs of very early date ; and within the limits of the parish are the remains of the old castles of Cappa, Castle Crine, Mountcashel, and Ballycullen ; those of the last are extensive, and some vestiges of the outworks are still visible ; and those of Mountcashel stand on an eminence near a lake, which thence takes its name.-See **SIX-MILE-BRIDGE.**

KILHENY, or **KILLEANY,** a parish, in the barony of **BURREN,** county of **CLARE,** and province of **MUNSTER,** about 11 miles (S. W.) from Burren, near the road from Ballyvaughan to Ballyaline bay; containing 465 inhabitants. It is the estate of the Creagh family, by patent of Chas. II., and comprises 3111 statute acres, consisting chiefly of rocky mountain pasture, but containing some very rich grazing farms, from which large droves of cattle are sent to Cork and Liverpool. About two feet below the surface is a stratum of excellent limestone, causing very great productiveness in the soil, which, on the townland of Ballyconroe South, has been known to yield nine crops in succession without manuring. It is a rectory and vicarage, in the diocese of Kilfenora, forming part of the union of Kilcorney, and the corps of the chancellorship of the cathedral of Kilfenora : the tithes amount to £25. In the R. C. divisions it forms part of the union or district of Tuoclea, or Arranview, and has a small chapel at Toumavara, in which a school of about 50 scholars is kept. Here are the ruins of a chapel, the burial-ground of which is still used; five forts, called Cahers, composed of huge blocks of limestone, with underground apartments ; a cromlech ; and a cave called *Poul Ilva,* more than 150 feet in depth, at the bottom of which is seen a subterranous stream, which, after a course of about two miles, appears above ground near the old parish church.

KILKEE, or **DOOGH,** a village, in the parish of **KILFIERAGH,** barony of **MOYARTA,** county of **CLARE,** and province of **MUNSTER,** 61/2 miles (W. by N.) from Kilrush, on the western coast ; containing 1051 inhabitants. In 1831 it consisted of 153 houses ; since which time several houses and bathing lodges have been erected, the village being much frequented as a bathing-place, chiefly by the citizens of Limerick, on account of its remarkably fine strand, which is sheltered by a ledge of rocks stretching across one-third of Kilkee bay. There are tepid baths, the property of Jonas Studdart, Esq. It has a penny post to Kilrush, and is a constabulary police station and a coast-guard station, the latter being one of the six within the district of Miltown-Malbay. Petty sessions are held every Friday, and a court for the recovery of small debts is occasionally held for the manor of Kilrush. It is in contemplation to establish fairs in May and August. Divine worship is performed in a lodge, but subscriptions are being collected for the erection of a new parochial church. A handsome and spacious R. C. chapel has been lately built, and there are a parochial school, and a dispensary.-See **KILFIERAGH.**

KILKEEDY, or **KILKEADY**, a parish, in the barony of **INCHIQUIN**, county of **CLARE,** and province of **MUNSTER**, 6 miles (N. E.) from Curofin, on the road to Gort ; containing 3321 inhabitants. It is situated on the confines of the county, and comprises 15,390 statute acres, as applotted under the tithe act, a large portion of which is rough mountain pasture. There are several lakes, of which Lough Buneagh is of considerable extent. The principal seats are Rockforest, the residence of Bindon Blood, Esq., situated in a finely planted demesne extending nearly a mile along the road ; Rockvale, of J. D'Arcy, Esq. ; Carrignagoule, of J. Roughan, Esq. ; Ratope, of the late J. Foster, Esq. ; and Derryowen, of C. Lobdell, Esq. Fairs are held at Turraghmore on the 8th of June, and at Tubber on July 12th and Sept. 20th, chiefly for cattle ; the first is numerously attended. Petty sessions are held at Derryowen every alternate week, and a court for the manor of Inchiquin is held occasionally for the recovery of small debts. The parish is in the diocese of Killaloe : the rectory is partly appropriate to the prebend of Tomgrany, in the cathedral of Killaloe, partly impropriate in the representatives of the Right Hon. James Fitzgerald, and partly united with the vicarage, which forms part of the union of Kilneboy. The tithes amount to £144. 4. 0$\frac{1}{4}$., of which £9. 15. 5. is payable to the prebendary, £13. 18. 11$\frac{1}{2}$. to the impropriators, and £120. 19. 6$\frac{3}{4}$. to the vicar. The church is a small plain edifice, without tower or spire. The R. C. parish is co-extensive with that of the Established Church, and contains a large chapel at Boston, and a smaller one at Tubber.

There is a school under the superintendence of the R. C. clergyman, in which are about 120 children. There are some remains of the castles of Rockvale, Fidane, Carrignagoule, Ratope, Derryowen, and Kilkeedy : the castle of Fidane is nearly perfect ; that of Derryowen was a square tower, 116 feet high, with very spacious rooms, but part of it has fallen.

KILKISHEN, a village, in the parish of **CLONLEA**, barony of **TULLA**, county of **CLARE**, and province of **MUNSTER**, 4 1/2 miles (N.) from Six-mile-bridge, on the road from that place to Tulla; containing 519 inhabitants. It consists of one main street of about 90 houses, and has a constabulary police station. Fairs are held on March 19th, Aug. 31st, and Dec. 22d. The church, the glebe-house, and the R. C. chapel of the parish, are here. Adjoining the village is Kilkishen, the seat of T. Studdert, Esq., in whose demesne are the remains of Kilkishen castle, consisting of a lofty square tower of great strength.-See **CLONLEA**.

KILLALOE, is a post-town and parish, and the seat of a diocese, in the barony of **TULLA**, county of **CLARE**, and province of **MUNSTER**, 20 miles (E. by S.) from Ennis, and 87 (S. W. by W.) from Dublin, on the road from Scariff to Nenagh ; containing 8587 inhabitants, of which number 1411 are in the town. This place, anciently called *Laonia*, derived its present name, supposed to be a corruption of *Kill-da-Lua*, from the foundation of an abbey, in the 6th century, by St. Lua or Molua, grandson of Eocha Baildearg, King of Munster, and which became the head of a diocese. Turlogh O'Brien, in 1054, built a bridge across the Shannon at this place, which had grown into some importance, though little of its previous history is related ; and, in 1061, Hugh O'Connor destroyed the castle which had been erected here, and burned the town, which was again reduced to ashes in 1080 and 1084, by the people of Conmacne. In 1177, Raymond Le Gros, after his triumphant entry into Limerick, came to this place, where he received the hostages of Roderic, King of Connaught, and O'Brien, Prince of Thomond, who took the oath of fealty to the King of England. On Richard de Clare's obtaining a grant of certain lands in the county of Clare, this town, as containing the only ford over the Shannon, obtained for some time the appellation of Claresford. In 1367, after the recall of "Lionel", Duke of Clarence, from the government of Ireland, who had acquired considerable tracts of territory around the town, Murrogh-na-Ranagh, one of the O'Briens, made himself master of all the country beyond the Shannon, and destroyed this town and several others belonging to the English. Gen. Sarsfield, in 1681, posted a strong party at this place, to defend the passage of the river ; but having abandoned their post, the English advanced into the western provinces ; and in 1691 the same general, at the head of a select body of cavalry, passed the river and destroyed a convoy of ammunition on its way to Wm. III., then at Limerick.

The town is pleasantly situated on a rising ground on the western bank of the Shannon, near the noted falls of Killaloe, and about a mile from Lough Derg, and is connected with the county of Tipperary by an ancient bridge of nineteen arches. It consists of one square, and a principal and several smaller streets, and contains about 300 houses. There is a small infantry barrack. A flourishing trade in stuffs, camlets, and serges was formerly carried on, and two well-supplied markets were held weekly ; but both the manufacture and the markets have been discontinued. Above and below the bridge there are numerous eel weirs, which produce a strong current in the river, and there is also a salmon fishery. In the vicinity are some very extensive slate quarries, from which, on an average, about 100,000 tons are annually raised for the supply of the surrounding country to a great distance. A mill, with machinery driven by water, has been erected at an expense of £6000, for cutting and polishing stone and marble, and working them into mantel-pieces, flags, slabs, and other articles, in which about 100 men are employed, and for whose residence near the works are some handsome slated cottages. A spirit of cheerful industry and enterprise seems to promise much for the increasing prosperity of the town. Close to these mills is a yard for boat-building, belonging to the Shannon Steam Navigation Company, whose head-quarters are at this place, and who have established a regular communication by steam-packets, for goods and passengers, up the Shannon, through Lough Derg to Portumna, Athlone, and Banagher, and from Banagher by canal-boats to Dublin. The company afford employment to a great number of persons in the construction and repair of docks and ware-houses. About a quarter of a mile from the village of O'Brien's Bridge is the pier-head, where the steam-boats transfer their cargoes and passengers to a packet-boat, which is towed at a rapid rate to Limerick, between which place and Dublin packet-boats ply daily ; the trip to Portumna and Williamstown is beautifully picturesque. Below the bridge the navigation of the Shannon is interrupted by a ridge of rocks, over which the water rushes with great noise ; and the appearance of the town at this place, with the waters of Lough Derg in the distance, and its venerable cathedral rising above the bridge and backed by a fine mountain range, is strikingly romantic. To remedy this obstruction of the navigation, the Board of Inland Navigation constructed a canal through the bishop's demesne, avoiding the rocks, and joining the river beyond the falls ; it has also erected an hotel, called Ponsonby Arms, for the accommodation of families visiting Lough Derg and its neighbourhood. This lake is about thirty miles in length, and abounds with beautiful and interesting scenery, more especially in that part which is near the town ; the shores are embellished with several handsome mansions, embosomed in luxuriant woods and plantations, and with several ancient and venerable castles. Pike, perch, trout, and various other fish are taken in abundance, among which is found the Gillaroo trout. Fairs are held on April 5th, May 24th, Sept. 3rd and Oct. 20th ; and petty sessions once a fortnight. A constabulary police force is stationed in the town.

The SEE of KILLALOE was originally founded about 639, by Pope John IV., who consecrated St. Flannan, successor to St. Lua or Molua, first bishop. Theodrick, King of Munster and father of St. Flannan, endowed the see with many estates, and was interred in the abbey. Moriertach, King of Ireland, and Donald O'Brien, King of Limerick, were also great benefactors ; and the former was interred here with great pomp in 1120. The church early became a favourite place of resort for pilgrims, and among numerous others was Connor Mac Dermod O'Brien, King of Thomond and Desmond, who died here on a pilgrimage in 1142. The cathedral was erected by Donald, King of Limerick, in 1160. About the close of this century the ancient bishoprick of Roscrea was permanently united to this see, together with a portion of that of Iniscathay ; and in 1752 the see of Kilfenora, which had been founded by St. Fachnan, was also united to it ; and the two dioceses have, since that period, been always held together. It is one of the twelve dioceses that constitute the ecclesiastical province of Cashel, and comprehends parts of the Queen's county, Limerick, Galway, and King's county, with a large portion of the county of Tipperary, and the greater part of Clare ; it extends about 100 miles in length, varying from 9 to 32 in breadth, and comprises an estimated superfices of 628,500 acres, of which 3200 are in Queen's county, 5300 in Limerick, 8800 in Galway, 50,000 in King's county, 134,500 in Tipperary, and 426,700 in Clare. The lands belonging to the see comprise 7528 statute acres, of which 6795 are profitable land ; and the gross revenue, on an average of three years ending Dec. 31st, 1831, amounted to £4532. 9. 1. Since that time the dioceses of Clonfert and Kilmacduagh, having become vacant, have been, under the Church Temporalities' Act of the 3d of Will. IV., united to the see of Killaloe, and the temporalities vested in the Ecclesiastical Commissioners. The chapter consists of a dean, precentor, chancellor, treasurer, and archdeacon ; there are also seven prebenderies, who have no voice in the chapter, viz., those of Tomgranna, Lackeen, Clondgad, Dysert, Tulla, Inniscattery, and Rath. The consistorial court consists of a vicar-general, registrar, and proctor ; the registrar is keeper of the records, of which the earliest are of the date 1668, the old registry having been burnt during the parliamentary war. The total number of parishes in the diocese is 108, of which 89 are comprised in 41 unions, and 19 are single benefices, of which one is in the patronage of the crown, 11 in lay patronage, and 38 in that of the bishop. The number of churches is 56, and there are five other places in which divine service is performed ; and of glebe-houses, 39. The cathedral, which also serves for the parish church, is an ancient cruciform structure, with a square central tower ; it is about 200 feet in length, with a fine east window, and the west front has an imposing appearance ; the prevailing character is that of the Norman style. Near it is a building called the Oratory of St. Molua, one of the most ancient ecclestical edifices in the country, being apparently of the 7th century ; it was roofed with stone, but is now in ruins. The economy fund of the cathedral amounts to £602. 10. 5. per annum. In the R. C. divisions, the dioceses of Kilfenora is held with Kilmacduagh ; the diocese of Killaloe is co-extensive with that of the Established Church, and is an independent bishoprick. The number of benefices, or unions, is 49, and of chapels 111, which are served by 123 clergymen, of whom 49 are parish priests, and 79 are coadjutors or curates.

The parish comprises 13,045 statute acres, and is generally under profitable cultivation. The surrounding scenery is beautifully diversified, and in many parts truly picturesque. Near the town, on the west bank of the Shannon, is Clarrisford House, the episcopal palace, finely situated in a highly improved demesne, near the only ford across the river into this county from that of Tipperary ; the mansion is handsome and of modern appearance, and, those small, forms a pleasant residence. There are several gentlemen's seats, most of which command fine views of the lake and the beautiful scenery along its shores : of these, the principal are Ballyvalley, the residence of W. Parker, Esq., from which is a fine view of the town and bridge, with the falls on the river: Tinerana, of S. G. Purdon, Esq., Ryhinch, of Jeremiah O' Brien, Esq. ; Derry Castle, of Capt. Head ; Castle Lough, of Anthony Parker, Esq. ; Youghall, of William Smithwick, Esq., and Ogonilloe, of the Rev. R. W. Nisbett. The living is a perpetual curacy, in the patronage of the Dean and Chapter ; the rectory is appropriate to the economy fund of the cathedral : the tithes amount to £369. 4. 7$1/2$., of which £295. 7. 8$1/2$. is payable to the economy fund, and £73. 15. 11. to the bishop, as mensal tithes ; the stipend of the curate is £60 per annum, paid out of the economy fund. The R. C. parish is co-extensive with that of the Established Church ; there are four chapels, also a place of worship for Presbyterians. About 110 children are taught in a public school, and there are seven private schools, in which are about 400 children. Near the town is a rath, where was formerly the castle or palace of Brien Boroihme, monarch of all Ireland : this fort, called *Ceanchora* or *Kinkora*, was destroyed by Domohall Mac Adgail, Prince of Tyrconnell, during the absence of Murtogh, grandson of Brien ; the site has been levelled and planted, and few vestiges of the original building can be traced.

KILLARD, a parish, in the barony of **IBRICKANE**, county of **CLARE**, and province of **MUNSTER**, 7 miles (N. W.) from Kilrush, on the road from Kilkee to Miltown-Malbay ; containing 5619 inhabitants. This parish, which is on the western coast, and includes the cliff of Baltard, comprises 8824 statute acres, as applotted under the tithe act : there is a large quantity of reclaimable bog and rocky land ; the system of agriculture is improving. Slate and flag quarries exist here. Very fine salmon is caught in Dunbeg river ; and the banks of Baltard, about three leagues from the shore, afford turbot, cod, haddock, doree, mackerel, whiting, and other fish, in great abundance and perfection. The coast being very precipitous and the surf great, the fishermen use canoes of wicker work covered with pitched canvas. Baltard House is the residence of the Rev. M. Comyn, P. P. The living is a vicarage, in the diocese of Killaloe, and in the patronage of the Bishop ; the rectory is impropriate in the representatives of Lord Castlecoote and in R. Stackpoole, Esq. The tithes amount to £208. 19. 9., of which £85. 14. 2. is payable to the representatives of Lord Castlecoote, £13. 4. 7. to R. Stackpoole, Esq., and the remainder to the vicar. The church is a modern building near Dunbeg. In the R. C. divisions this parish forms part of the union or district of Kilkee, and has a chapel at Dunbeg. A parochial school has been established under the patronage of the incumbent and Mr. Straight, the latter of whom gave the school-house and a piece of ground rent-free ; there is also a school partly supported by the parish priest. In these schools are about 70, and in four private schools about 340, children. On the summit of Baltard cliff are the ruins of a signal tower ; and on the south-western side of Dunbeg bay are the ruins of Dunmore castle ; and there are some remains of the old church.-See **DUNBEG.**

KILLASPUGLENANE, a parish, in the barony of **CORCOMROE,** county of **CLARE,** and province of **MUNSTER,** 2¾ miles (N. W.) from Ennistymon, on the western coast ; containing 1454 inhabitants. It comprises 2943 statute acres, as applotted under the tithe act, consisting chiefly of coarse mountain pasture. Here is Moymore, the residence of - Stackpoole, Esq. It is a vicarage, in the diocese of Kilfenora, forming part of the union of Kilmanaheen ; the rectory forms part of the corps of the archdeaconry of Kilfenora, and the tithes amount to £105, of which £75 is payable to the archdeacon, and £30 to the vicar : there is a glebe of two acres. In the R. C. divisions it is part of the union or district of Liscanor, and has a plain chapel at Cahirgal. Some remains of the old church still exist.

KILLEANY, county of CLARE.-See **KILHENY.**

KILLEANY, barony of CLARE, county of GALWAY.-See **KILLENY.**

KILLEILAGH, a parish, in the barony of **CORCOMROE**, county of **CLARE**, and province of **MUNSTER**, 61/4 miles (N. W. by N.) from Ennistymon, on the road from Ballyvaughan to Ballyaline. This parish comprises 11,332 statute acres, a large part of which consists of mountain pasture and bog. Slate of inferior quality is found at Donagore. Ballyaline Bay is well situated for fishing, and has a coast-guard station, included in the Miltown-Malbay district ; and there is a constabulary police station at Knockfin. Off the coast is Innishere, one of the Arran isles, between which and the mainland is the South Sound, or entrance to Galway bay. The principal seats are Doolen, the residence of Major W. N. McNamara ; Arranview, of F. McNamara, Esq., commanding, as its name implies, a fine view of the Arran isles and the coast of Galway ; and Ballyaline, of F. Gore, Esq. ; besides which there are several other respectable residences. It is a vicarage, in the diocese of Kilfenora, forming part of the union of Kilmanaheen ; the rectory is united to those of Kilmoon and Carrune. The tithes amount to £221. 10. 9., of which £147. 13. 10. is payable to the rector, and £73. 16. 11. to the vicar. The church is in ruins. In the R. C. divisions it is part of the union or district of Arranview, or Tuoclea, and has a chapel at Knockfin. There are one public and three private schools. At Glassie, and Donagore, are the ruins of the castles respectively so called, the latter being a circular tower on a square base ; and at Ballynalacken, on a rocky eminence near the sea, stands the castle of that name, which is about to be repaired by J. O'Brien, Esq. its proprietor. Boetius Clancy, a celebrated chieftain, formerly resided at St. Catherine's where a mound of earth is still shown as the spot where his castle once stood.

KILLELY, or **KILLEELY,** partly within the north liberties of the city of **LIMERICK**, but chiefly in the barony of **BUNRATTY**, county of **CLARE**, and province of **MUNSTER**, 3 miles (N. W.) from Limerick, on the mail road to Ennis, and on the river Shannon ; containing 5141 inhabitants. This parish, which is also called Meelick, comprises 5135 statute acres, as applotted under the tithe act, which are nearly equally divided between tillage and pasture. It extends nearly to the old Thomond bridge, at Limerick, and includes the extensive distillery of Messrs. Brown, Stein, and Co. Limestone abounds and is used for manure, and there is some bog near the Shannon. There are stations of the constabulary police at Cratloe, Meelick, and Thomond Gate. Cratloe House is the residence of Stafford O'Brien, Esq. ; the demesne and wood of Cratloe, which are chiefly in this parish, extend into the adjoining parish of Kilfentinan. The living is a rectory and vicarage, in the diocese of Limerick, and in the patronage of the Bishop : the tithes amount to £281. 1. 11½. The church, a small plain structure, is picturesquely situated at Meelick ; it was built by the grandmother of the present Marquess of Conyngham, and subsequently made parochial ; it is now undergoing a thorough repair, a grant of £220 having been made by the Ecclesiastical Commissioners for that purpose. The communion plate was presented by the Conyngham family. The glebe-house, a large mansion, commanding a beautiful view of the Shannon, stands on a glebe of 11½ acres. In the R. C. divisions this parish is partly in the district of Meelick, and partly in that of Thomond Gate, or St. Lelia. In the parochial school, supported by the rector, about 20 children are educated ; and about 80 females are taught in a public school supported by subscription : there are also four private schools, containing about 170 children, and a Sunday school is held in the parochial school-house. About one mile south-east from Cratloe Cross is the Cratloe and Meelick public dispensary.

KILLEYMUR, or **KILLIMER**, a parish, in the barony of **CLONDERLAW**, county of **CLARE**, and province of **MUNSTER**, 4 miles (E. S. E.) from Kilrush, on the river Shannon ; containing 3023 inhabitants. It comprises 4621 statute acres, as applotted under the tithe act, and is principally under tillage. The land is generally good, and there is a small quantity of bog ; sea-weed is used as manure. Flags of superior quality are quarried at Money-Point. The principal seats are Burrane House, the residence of J. Hodges, Esq. ; Donogrogue Castle, of G. Crowe Hodges, Esq. ; Caradole of R. D. Daxon, Esq. ; and Besborough, of the Rev. Theobald Butler. It is a vicarage, in the diocese of Killaloe, forming part of the union of Kilmurry-Clonderlaw ; the rectory is partly impropriate in the representatives of Lord Castlecoote, and partly forms a portion of the rectorial union of Kilrush. The tithes amount to £203. 1. 6½., of which £55. 7. 8¼. is payable to the rector of Kilrush, £64. 12. 3¾. to the impropriator, and £83. 1. 6½. to the vicar : there is a glebe of one acre. In the R. C. divisions it forms part of the union or district of

Kilrush, and contains a chapel, in which is a school of about 100 children. There is also a private school, in which about 30 children are taught. The ruins of the parish church, and of another small church or chapel still exist.

KILLOFIN, a parish, in the barony of **CLONDERLAW**, county of **CLARE**, and province of **MUNSTER**, 7 miles (S. W.) from Kildysart, on the river Shannon ; containing 4073 inhabitants. It comprises 3948 statute acres, and is almost entirely under tillage, yielding abundant crops ; there is some bog. In several parts of the parish are indications of coal, and culm is obtained at Slievedooly and Clonkerry. The south-western part of the parish consists of a peninsula, projecting into the Shannon, and forming the south-east side of Clonderlaw bay. On Kilkeran Point, at its extremity, is a battery mounting six 24-pounders and two howitzers, with a bomb-proof barrack for a detachment of artillerymen. The principal seats are Ballyartney, the residence of R. Barclay, Esq. ; Clonkerry, of T. Lloyd, Esq. ; and Kilkeran Lodge, the property of T. Spaight, Esq. It is a vicarage, in the diocese of Killaloe, forming part of the union of Kilmurry-Clonderlaw : the rectory is impropriate in Bindon Scott, Esq. : the tithes amount to £284, of which £160 is payable to the impropriator, and £124 to the vicar. In the R. C. divisions it is also part of the union or district of Kilmurry-Clonderlaw, and has a handsome cruciform chapel near Labasheeda. There are six private schools, in which about 420 children are educated. Some remains of the parish church still exist, the burial-ground of which is still used ; at Kilkerin are the ruins of a small church, with a burial-ground, which is only used for the interment of children ; and at Killanna are the ruins of an ancient building, supposed to have been a monastery. In Millpark is a chalybeate spring.-See **LABASHEEDA**.

KILLOKENNEDY, a parish, in the barony of **TULLA**, county of **CLARE**, and province of **MUNSTER**, 5 miles (W.) from Killaloe, on the road from that place to Ennis ; containing 3586 inhabitants. It comprises 9,349 statute acres, as applotted under the tithe act, including much mountain pasture and some bog. Good building and flag stone are obtained. Ballyquin, the seat of - Arthur, Esq., is situated in Glenomera, which is celebrated as a shooting station for grouse and pheasants. At Kilbane is a constabulary police station. It is a vicarage, in the diocese of Killaloe, forming part of the union of Kiltonanlea, or Doonass : the rectory is part of the union of Omullod : the tithes amount to £216. 2. 9$_{1/2}$. per annum, of which £106. 3. 1. is payable to the vicar, and the remainder to the rector. In the R. C. divisions it forms part of the unions or districts of Broadford and Doonass, and has chapels at Kilbane and Kilmore. There are two private schools, in which about 220 children are educated.

KILLONE, or **KILLOWEN**, a parish, in the barony of **ISLANDS**, county of **CLARE**, and province of **MUNSTER**, 2$_{1/2}$ miles (S. by W.) from Ennis, on the road to Kildysart ; containing 2354 inhabitants. It comprises about 3,820 statute acres, as rated for the county cess. Limestone abounds, and is used for manure, for which purpose sea-weed and sand from the shores of the Fergus are also used ; and the state of agriculture is gradually improving. About the year 1190, Donald O'Brien, King of Limerick, founded an abbey here for nuns of the order of St. Augustine, and dedicated it to St. John the Baptist. Slaney, the pious daughter of Donogh Carbreach, King of Thomond, was abbess of this nunnery. The ruins are beautifully situated near the north-eastern extremity of the Lake of Killone, and form a very picturesque feature in the scenery. At a short distance from the abbey is a celebrated holy well, dedicated to St. John, on the eve of whose anniversary it is resorted to by the peasantry from various parts of the county. The principal seats are, Edenvale, the residence of R. J. Stackpoole, Esq. ; and New Hall, of J. McDonnell, Esq. : both are situated in picturesque demesnes, the latter being on an eminence above the Lake of Killone, and the former celebrated for its romantic vale, in which is a secluded lake, said to communicate with the river Fergus by a subterraneous channel. The parish is in the diocese of Killaloe : the rectory is impropriate in Bindon Scott, Esq., who receives the tithes, amounting to £180, and allows £10 per annum late currency for discharging the clerical duties ; but the townland of Bearnageehy pays tithes to the rector of Clare Abbey. In the R. C. divisions it forms part of the union or district of Clare, and has a chapel at Ballyea. About 170 children are educated in two private schools.

KILLONOGHAN, or **KILLONAHON**, a parish, in the barony of **BURREN**, county of **CLARE**, and province of **MUNSTER**, 13 miles (S. W.) from Burren, on the western coast ; containing 1185 inhabitants. This parish consists principally of rocky mountain pasture, affording scanty but rich herbage ; a detached portion is situated at some distance to the south-east, and another portion is isolated by the parish of Glaninagh. Lead is found in the vicinity of Glenvaan, and it is supposed that a vein extends into the limestone hills of Burren. It is a rectory and vicarage, in the diocese of Kilfenora, forming part of the union of Dromcrehy, or Rathbourney, and the corps of the treasurership of the cathedral of Kilfenora : the tithes amount to £82. 10. In the R. C. divisions it is part of the union or district of Glynn, or Glenarragha, and has a chapel at Stone-hall. About 50 children are educated in a private school. There are some remains of the old church, near which are the ruins of a castle, which consisted of a round tower.

KILLURANE, a parish, in the barony of **TULLA**, county of **CLARE**, and province of **MUNSTER**, 61/4 miles (N. W. by W.) from Killaloe, on the road from Broadford to Tulla ; containing 2959 inhabitants. It comprises 3197 statute acres, as applotted under the tithe act, of which about 440 are mountain pasture and bog, and the remainder arable land ; part of Doon lake is also in this parish. The manufacture of hair-cloth and coarse carpets is carried on to a small extent at Bally-McDonnell. The principal seats are Derrimore, the residence of F. Gore, Esq. ; Doon, of the Rev. W. Butler ; and Elm Hill, of J. Bentley, Esq. It is a vicarage, in the diocese of Killaloe, forming part of the union of Kilseily ; the rectory is appropriate to the prebend of Tomgrany and the union of Omullod. The tithes amount to £204. 1. 8., of which £78. 5. 61/2. is payable to the incumbent of Omullod, £33. 10. to the prebendary, and the remainder to the vicar. In the R. C. divisions it is part of the union or district of Kilkishene, and has a chapel at Callaghans-Mills, *which see*. There are ruins of ancient castles at Monegona, Tierovane, and on the shore of the lake of Doon.

KILMACDUANE, a parish, in the barony of **MOYARTA**, county of **CLARE**, and province of **MUNSTER**, 53/4 miles (N. by E.) from Kilrush, on the road to Miltown-Malbay ; containing 5738 inhabitants. It comprises 9735 statute acres, as applotted under the tithe act, of which a large portion consists of hilly pasture and bog. Fairs are held at Cooreclare, or Conclare, on May 6th, June 4th and 26th, July 10th, Oct. 20th, and Dec. 20th, for general farming stock. A court is occasionally held there by the seneschal for the manor of Kilrush, at which small debts are recoverable ; and it is also a station of the constabulary police. Dromelly is the residence of J. O'Brien, Esq. The townland of Gurrantuohy, though entirely isolated by the parish of Kilrush, belongs to this parish. It is a vicarage, in the diocese of Killaloe, forming part of the union of Kilmurry-Clonderlaw ; the rectory is impropriate in the representatives of Lord Castlecoote. The tithes amount to £304. 12. 3¾., of which £184. 12. 3¾. is payable to the impropriators, and the remainder to the vicar. The townlands of Cahirfeenich and Acres are exempt from the payment of rectorial tithes. In the R. C. divisions it forms part of the union or district of Kilmihill, or Kilmichael : there are chapels at Cooreclare and Creegh. In six private schools about 220 children are educated. The ruins of the old church still remain.

KILMACREHY, a parish, in the barony of **CORCOMROE**, county of **CLARE**, and province of **MUNSTER**, 4 miles (W.) from Ennistymon, on the north side of Liscanor bay on the western coast ; containing 3343 inhabitants. Within its limits is the headland called Hag's Head, a lofty basaltic promontory situated in lat. 52° 16' 40", and lon. 9° 25' 20" ; from this point the cliffs gradually ascend to Moher, where they attain their greatest elevation, and are estimated to be about 600 feet above the level of the sea. The waves here break with tremendous force against the rocks ; part of the Spanish Armada was, in 1588, wrecked on the shore. On the most elevated point of these stupendous cliffs an ornamental building in the castellated style is now being erected by Cornelius O'Brien, Esq., for the accommodation of visiters to this bold and iron-bound coast, from which is obtained a magnificent view embracing nearly the whole line of coast from Loop Head to the northern extremity of the bay of Galway, together with the Arran Isles and a vast expanse of the Atlantic Ocean. Puffins are taken here by persons who are suspended over the lofty precipices, in the cavities of which these birds deposit their young. The parish comprises 5492 statute acres, as applotted under the tithe act, of which a considerable portion consists of mountain pasture : the arable land is generally manured with sea weed and sand, and the state of agriculture is generally improving. The gentlemen's seats are Birchfield, the residence of Cornelius O'Brien, Esq., who has much improved his estate and the condition of his tenantry by the erection of neat slated cottages and farm-buildings, and by other judicious arrangements ; and Moher, of J. MacNamara, Esq. The parish is in the diocese of Kilfenora : the rectory forms part of the corps of the archdeaconry, and the vicarage part of the union of Kilmanaheen, in the gift of the Bishop. The tithes amount to £230. 15. 5$3/4$., and there is a glebe of 2$1/2$ acres. In the R. C. divisions it forms part of the union or district of Liscanor, which also includes the parish of Killaspuglenane ; the chapel is at Liscanor, and there is also a chapel for the rural district : near the former is a school. The ruins of the ancient church retain several fine specimens of arches and mouldings now imbedded in the walls. At Dough and Liscanor are the ruined castles respectively so called ; and near Birchfield is a holy well, dedicated to St. Bridget, and much resorted to by the peasantry, which, at Mr. O'Brien's expense, has been surrounded by tasteful plantations and rustic seats, and at the entrance is a neat lodge.-See **LISCANOR**.

KILMALEERY, a parish, in the barony of **BUNRATTY**, county of **CLARE**, and province of **MUNSTER**, 1 mile (S. W.) from Newmarket, on the east bank of the river Fergus ; containing 667 inhabitants. It comprises 2360 statute acres, as applotted under the tithe act. The land is in general of superior quality, particularly on the shore of the Fergus, where it is exceedingly rich. At Carrigeary is a small quay, where turf and sea manure are landed, and whence corn is occasionally sent to Limerick ; and at Cahirvane is the ancient seat of James Creagh, Esq. The parish is in the diocese of Killaloe ; the rectory forms part of the rectorial union of Tomfinlough or Tradree, and the vicarage part of the vicarial union of Kilnasoolagh. The tithes amount to £126. 0. 3$3/4$., of which £73. 16. 11. is payable to the rector, and the remainder to the vicar. In the R. C. Divisions it is part of the union or district of Newmarket, and has a chapel at Carrigeary. The ruined castles of Urlin and Clenagh still remain ; the latter, a lofty square tower nearly entire, was once the residence of the MacMahons.

KILMALY, a parish, in the barony of **ISLANDS**, county of **CLARE**, and province of **MUNSTER**, 4$1/2$ miles (W. S. W.) from

Ennis, on the mountain road to Miltown Malbay ; containing 4296 inhabitants. It comprises 22,584 statute acres, about one-half of which consists of coarse mountain pasture and bog, and the remainder of arable land of various quality : the state of agriculture is gradually improving. Fairs are held at Cornally on Jan. 2nd, April 17th, July 18th, and Oct. 3rd. Lough Burke, the ancient seat of the family of Burke, and now occupied by the Lucas family, is picturesquely situated on the lake to which it gives name. The living is a rectory and vicarage, in the diocese of Killaloe : the rectory forms part of the rectorial union of Dromcliffe, and the vicarage (separated in 1832 from the vicarial union of Dromcliffe) now forms a separate benefice, in the gift of the Bishop. The tithes amount to £203. 1. 61/2., of which £129. 4. 7. is payable to the rector, and £73. 16. 11. to the vicar. There is no church or glebe-house, but divine service is regularly performed in a licensed house at Gortnaganiff, which is also used as a school-house. In the R. C. divisions the parish forms part of the union or district of Inch, or West Dromcliffe ; there are chapels at Kilmaly and Cornally. In the public school at Gortnaganiff about 30, and in two private schools about 150, children are educated. On every hill in this parish (nearly 30 in number) is an ancient fort or rath : the ruins of the old church are still to be seen in the burial-ground.

KILMANAHEEN, a parish, in the barony of **CORCOMROE**, county of **CLARE**, and province of **MUNSTER**, on the road from Ennis to Miltown-Malbay ; containing, with the post-town of Ennistymon and the village of Lahinch (both of which are separately described), 5475 inhabitants. It comprises 8545 statute acres, of which a large portion consists of hilly pasture, and from its situation on the bay of Liscanor, the portion under tillage is manured with sea weed and sand, which is here procured in abundance : the state of agriculture is gradually improving. The principal seats are Ennistymon House, the residence of A. Finucane, Esq. ; the glebe-house, of the Ven. Archdeacon Whitty ; Lahenzy, the property of A. Stackpoole, Esq. ; Woodmount, of G. F. Lysaght, Esq. ; and Moy, the occasional residence of Sir W. Fitzgerald, Bart. The living is a rectory and vicarage, in the diocese of Kilfenora ; the rectory is united to those of Kilmacrehy and Killaspuglenane, constituting the corps of the archdeaconry ; and their respective vicarages, together with those of Killeilagh and Kilmoon, form the union of Kilmanaheen, in the patronage of the Bishop. The tithes of this parish amount to £254. 2. 11₁/₂., the entire tithes of the archdeaconry to £393. 5. 7., and those of the vicarial union to £295. 1. 11₁/₂. The glebe-house is a modern building, towards the erection of which the late Board of First Fruits contributed a loan of £369 and a gift of a similar sum, in 1828 : there is a glebe of 43 acres, subject to a charge of £10 per ann. late currency. The church at Ennistymon, built in 1831, is also a handsome structure, for the erection of which the same Board granted a loan of £1000. In the R. C. divisions the parish forms part of the union or district of Ennistymon, which also comprises the parish of Clouney, and contains the chapels of Ennistymon, Lahinch, and Kilthomas. In the public schools at Ennistymon about 340 children are educated, and there are also in the parish nine private schools. The ruins of the old church still remain in the burial-ground.

KILMIHILL, or **KILMICHAEL,** a parish, in the barony of **CLONDERLAW,** county of **CLARE,** and province of **MUNSTER,** 8 miles (W. N. W.) from Kildysart, on the road from Kilrush to Ennis ; containing 3794 inhabitants, of which number, 79 are in the hamlet. It comprises 8089 statute acres, as applotted under the tithe act, about two-thirds of which consist of arable land of medium quality, and the remainder of mountain pasture : there is also a considerable portion of waste and bog. Fairs are held at the village on May 19th, July 18th, and Sept. 29th ; and a court for the manor of Crovreahan is occasionally held at Kilmichael by the seneschal, in which small debts are recoverable. The parish is in the diocese of Killaloe ; the rectory is impropriate in the representatives of Lord Castlecoote and John Scott, Esq., and the vicarage forms part of the union of Kilfarboy. The tithes amount to £192, of which £62. 15. 4₁/₂. is payable to Lord Castlecoote's representatives, £55. 7. 8₁/₂. to John Scott, Esq., and the remainder to the vicar. In the R. C. divisions it is the head of a union or district, which also comprises the parish of Kilmacduane, and contains the chapel of Kilmichael, and those of Cooreclare and Creegh in Kilmacduane. About 120 children are educated in two private schools. The ruins of the old church still remain in the burial-ground.

KILMOON, a parish, in the barony of **BURREN**, county of **CLARE**, and province of **MUNSTER**, 8 miles (N.) from Ennistymon, on the road from Ballyvaughan to the bay of Ballyhaline, containing 1088 inhabitants. This parish, which derives its name from an ancient conventual church of which no records are extant, comprises about 11,000 Irish statute acres, of which 5285 are applotted under the tithe act ; the remainder consists chiefly of rocky mountain and bog. With the exception only of the townlands of Lisdoonvarna and Ballytigue, which belong to the Stackpoole family, the whole of the parish, together with that of Kilheny or Killeany, and the Castle, town, and lands of Dangan in the barony of Bunratty, were granted by Chas. II. to Pierse Creagh, Esq., as a reward for his services against Cromwell, and in compensation for the loss of his estate of Adare, in the county of Limerick, great part of which are held, with the manorial rights and privileges, by his descendant, Pierse Creagh, Esq., of Rathbane. The surface is in general hilly and intersected by deep ravines formed by torrents rushing periodically from the mountain of Slieveilva, on the northern confines of the parish, one of the highest in the county, and celebrated for its abundance of grouse. Nearly two-thirds of the parish have a very rich substratum of limestone, lying about two feet beneath the surface, and producing most luxuriant herbage, highly prized for grazing cattle, of which large droves are sent to the Cork and Liverpool markets. Of the remainder, the greater part is dry bog covered with heath, which might be easily reclaimed and brought into cultivation, from the abundance and proximity of limestone. Very rich iron ore has been found in several places, and on the townland of Rathbane both coal and iron are stated to abound, though neither has yet been worked : slate also had been discovered on the mountain of Slieveilva. Rathbane is the residence of Pierse Creagh, Esq., who has greatly improved the ample and picturesque demesne in which it is situated ; large plantations have been made along the romantic glens, and on the banks of two beautiful rivulets which encircle the grounds. The living is a rectory and vicarage, in the diocese of Kilfenora, the rectory forming part of the union of Killeilagh, and the vicarage part of the union of Kilmanaheen : the tithes amount to £73. 16. 11., of which two-thirds are payable to the rector, and the remainder to the vicar. In the R. C. divisions the parish forms part of the union of Tuoclea. There are some slight remains of the convent, church, and cemetery of Kilmoon ; and within the limits of the parish are three large earthworks, and five stone forts called Cahers, said to have been Danish encampments. There are also considerable remains of the old castle of Lisdoonvarna, with its terraces, garden walls, and fortifications ; it was formerly the property of the Davorens, an ancient and powerful family in Burren, but now belongs to the Stackpoole family. On the demesne of Rathbane are several very powerful mineral springs, hitherto erroneously called the Lisdoonvarna spas, one of which is celebrated as being one of the strongest chalybeates in the kingdom : it contains so large a portion of iron, that in a few seconds it stains with a ferruginous colour any substance with which it may come in contact ; and has been found peculiarly efficacious in hepatitis, consumption, scorbutic and bilious affections, and rheumatism. Near this is another spring, which on analysis was found to contain, in addition to the iron, considerable portions of sulphur and magnesia ; the water is used with great benefit as an aperient. On the opposite side of a deep ravine, is a spring powerfully impregnated with naphtha, the exhalations of which taint the surrounding air ; silver thrown into the water is instantly changed to a deep gold colour ; and the water has been used with success as a cure for cutaneous diseases and for rheumatism. About a furlong further up the ravine, is a fourth spring, called the Copperas well ; it has not been analysed, but has been used externally from time immemorial with effect as a cure for ulcers. The Rathbane mineral springs, under the appellation of the Lisdoonvarna spas, have been known and appreciated for centuries ; they are situated in deep ravines at the base of lofty hills of black slate, between the strata of which are found large quantities of bright metallic ore resembling silver ; but from the bad state of the roads, and the want of proper accommodation, they have been comparatively neglected by invalids. Several cottages have, however, been recently built in the vicinity of these waters for the reception of visiters ; and if the proprietor continues his improvements, and a facility of access be afforded, this place will probably become one of the most frequented spas in Ireland.

KILMURRY-CLONDERLAW, a parish, in the barony of **CLONDERLAW**, county of **CLARE**, and province of **MUNSTER**, 7 miles (W. S. W.) from Kildysart, on the road to

Kilrush ; containing 3859 inhabitants. It is situated on the north-western side of the bay of Clonderlaw, and on the river Shannon. The bay is an open but insecure roadstead, near the bottom of which is a creek ; and at the village of Knock is a small pier for the convenience of boats landing sea manure and occasionally shipping grain to Limerick. The parish is estimated to comprise about 7380 statute acres, of which 6955 are applotted under the tithe act and mostly under tillage ; and from the abundant supply of rich manure afforded by the bay, the crops are very good : the state of agriculture has of late years been gradually improving. There is a large portion of bog, and in some places coal is supposed to exist, but has not yet been worked. Fairs are held at Kilmurry-McMahon on the 24th of May, July, and Sept. ; and a seneschal's court for Lord Egremont's manor of Clonderlaw is occasionally held, in which small debts are recoverable. The gentlemen's seats are Clonderlaw, that of G. Studdert, Esq. ; Kilmore, of Poole Hickman, Esq. ; Thornbury, of W. Studdert, Esq. ; Woodlawn, of Jos. Studdert, Esq. ; Oaklands, of R. Hunt, Esq. ; and Carabane, unoccupied. The living is a vicarage, in the diocese of Killaloe, episcopally united in 1774 to those of Killofin, Kilmacduane, Kilfedane, and Killeymur, together constituting the union of Kilmurry, in the patronage of the Bishop : the rectory is impropriate in John Scott, Esq. The tithes amount to £207. 13. 10$\frac{1}{4}$., of which £120 is payable to the impropriator, and the remainder to the vicar : the tithes of the entire benefice amount to £516. 6. 2. The glebe-house was built in 1811, when the late Board of First Fruits granted £450 as a gift and £53 as a loan towards its erection ; it is at present in indifferent repair. The glebe comprises 15 acres, subject to a rent of £3. 1. per acre ; and there is an old glebe of 1*a*. 3*r*. near the church. The church, built in 1810 on the site of the ancient edifice, and towards which the late Board granted a loan of £600, is a small plain structure with a square tower ; it is at present in a dilapidated state, but it is in contemplation by the Ecclesiastical Commissioners either to rebuild or thoroughly repair it. In the R. C. divisions this parish is the head of a union or district, which also includes the parish of Killofin, and contains the chapels of Kilmurry and Rhine : a spacious and handsome chapel is now in progress of erection at Dromdigus. The parochial school-house was built on the small glebe by the Rev. J. Martin, the present incumbent, aided by subscriptions and a grant from the Lord-Lieutenant's fund ; and a large public school has been lately established at Kilmurry McMahon : in these and in four private schools about 320 children are educated. In the demesne of Clonderlaw are the remains of a castle, formerly the residence of Sir Teigue McMahon.-See **KNOCK.**

KILMURRY-IBRICKANE, a parish, in the barony of **IBRICKANE**, county of **CLARE**, and province of **MUNSTER**, 4 miles (S.) from Miltown Malbay, on the road to Kilrush ; containing, with Mutton island or Enniskerry, 8433 inhabitants. It forms part of the dangerous western coast called "The Malbay," where if a vessel be embayed, its only chances of being saved are on the northern side of Liscanor bay, on the north-eastern side of Dunmore bay, or within the ledge of rocks opposite to Enniskerry, extending eastward from Seafield Point, in this parish. At each of these places a pier has been erected by the late Fishery Board ; that at Seafield can only be approached at spring tides by vessels of 12 tons' burden, but it is considered capable of being much improved, and would then be of great service. Here is a station of the coast-guard, being one of the six comprised in the district of Miltown-Malbay. The parish comprises 17,954 statute acres, as applotted under the tithe act, a large portion of which consists of mountain pasture and bog : the arable land is generally manured with sea-weed and sand, and the state of agriculture is gradually improving. A court is occasionally held at Tromaroe by the seneschal for the manor of Moih Ibrickane, in which small debts are recoverable. It is a rectory, in the diocese of Killaloe, entirely impropriate in the Earl of Egremont : the tithes amount to £184. 12. 33/4. In the R.C. divisions it forms part of the union or district of Miltown : there is a chapel of ease at Mullogh. In a school under the superintendence of the R. C. clergyman, and in six private schools, about 350 children are educated. The mountain streams in this parish form several picturesque cascades.-See **ENNISKERRY** and **MULLOGH.**

KILMURRYNEGAUL, a parish, in the barony of **TULLA**, county of **CLARE**, and province of **MUNSTER**, 23/4 miles (N. by W.) from Six-mile-bridge, on the road to Tulla ; containing 628 inhabitants. It comprises 2129 statute acres, as applotted under the tithe act, mostly under tillage : the state of agriculture has of late been much improved, chiefly through the exertions of T.

Studdert, Esq., of Kilkishen, whose residence, a handsome mansion surrounded by a well-wooded and highly improved demesne, is within the limits of this parish, and adjoining the village of Kilkishen, in the parish of Clonlea. It is in the diocese of Killaloe : the rectory forms part of the rectorial union of Ogashin, and the vicarage part of the union of Kilfinaghty. The tithes amount to £78. 9. 2₃/₄., of which £41. 10. 9₁/₄. is payable to the rector, and the remainder to the vicar. In the R. C. divisions it is part of the union or district of Six-mile-bridge, and has a chapel near the village of Kilmurry. The ruins of the old church still remain in the burial-ground, and within the limits of the parish are the ruined castles of Rossroe, Kilmurry, and Kilkishen ; the last stands in Mr. Studdert's demesne.

KILNASOOLAGH, a parish, in the barony of **BUNRATTY**, county of **CLARE**, and province of **MUNSTER**, adjoining the post-town of Newmarket-on-Fergus, on the road from Ennis to Limerick ; containing 1319 inhabitants. It comprises 5116 statute acres, as applotted under the tithe act ; the land is of excellent quality and mostly under tillage, and the state of agriculture has of late been much improved, chiefly through the exertions of Sir Edw. O'Brien, Bart. Limestone of superior quality abounds, some of which admits of a high polish. The Latoon river, which separates this parish from Quin on the north, is navigable to the bridge for lighters of 50 tons : sea manure is here landed, and corn is occasionally sent hence to Limerick. A cotton-manufactory was established a few years since, but was soon discontinued. The Newmarket petty sessions are held every alternate Thursday at Rathfoland, on the southern border of the parish, immediately adjoining the town. Dromoland, the seat of Sir Edw. O'Brien, Bart., is a superb edifice in the castellated style, lately erected on the site of the ancient mansion, and surrounded by an extensive and richly wooded demesne, in which great improvements have recently been made. On an eminence in the deer-park is a turret that forms a conspicuous land mark in the navigation of the Fergus. Carrigorin, the seat of Sir Wm. Fitzgerald, Bart., is a handsome mansion commanding a fine view of the junction of the Fergus and Shannon, and of the numerous islands by which the former is studded. The living is a vicarage, in the diocese of Killaloe, united to those of Dromline and Kilmaleery, and in the patronage of the Bishop : the rectory forms part of the rectorial union of Tradree or Tomfinlough. The tithes amount to £242. 1. 10₃/₄., of which £147. 13. 10₁/₄., is payable to the rector, and the remainder to the vicar : the entire tithes of the vicarial union amount to £184. 12. 4₁/₄. The glebe-house, erected about 1815, for which the late Board of First Fruits granted £400 as a gift and £260 as a loan, stands on a gentle eminence commanding an extensive prospect of the Fergus and Shannon and their numerous islands   the glebe comprises 12 acres, subject to a rent of £9 late currency, and there is a small glebe of 1₁/₄ acre near the church. The church, a large and handsome building with a tower surmounted by a spire, was rebuilt in 1815, at an expense of about £1500, towards which the same Board granted a loan of £900. It contains a finely executed monument to Sir Donat O'Brien, and some mural tablets of the Fitzgerald family. In the R. C. divisions the parish forms part of the union or district of Newmarket, where the principal chapel is situated. At Dromoland is a large school, with a garden and apartments for the master, entirely supported by the O'Brien family ; a female school is also supported by Lady O'Brien ; in these schools about 110 children are educated. There is also a small private school in the parish ; and the parochial school-house near the church, destroyed by accident some time since, is intended to be rebuilt by subscription. At Mohawn and Rathfoland are the ruins of the castles respectively so called.

KILNEBOY, a parish, in the barony of **INCHIQUIN**, county of **CLARE**, province of **MUNSTER** ; containing, with the post-town of Curofin (which is separately described), 3678 inhabitants. It is situated on the road from Ennis to Kilfenora, and comprises an extensive tract, of which about 6800 statute acres are assessed to the county rate ; a very large portion of the land is rocky pasture, a small proportion only being under tillage ; the soil varies from the poorest to the richest quality, resting on a substratum of limestone. There are some very extensive tracts of bog in the eastern portion of the parish ; coal has been discovered on the mountains of Clifden, lead ore at Glanquin, and a rich silver mine lately in Tullacommon, but none have been worked. The surface is boldly diversified and embellished with the picturesque lakes of Inchiquin and Tadune, the latter of which is but partly in the parish. The lake of Inchiquin is about 2₁/₂ miles in circumference, and is situated at the base of a richly wooded range of hills, forming a fine contrast to the bare limestone rocks in the vicinity. On its northern side are the interesting ruins of Inchiquin castle, from time immemorial the property and long the residence of the O'Brien family, whose descendant, the Marquess of Thomond, derives his title of Earl of Inchiquin from this estate ; they consist of a very ancient castle in a greatly dilapidated condition, and a mansion attached to it, and contribute much to the beautiful scenery of the lake. On the opposite shore is the mansion of the Burton family, the residence of E. W. Burton, Esq. ; and in the immediate vicinity of the lake are several seats, of which that called Adelphi is the elegant cottage residence of W. and F. Fitzgerald, Esqrs., adjoining which are the picturesque ruins of an old tower. An excellent road has been formed over the hill of Inchiquin from Adelphi to Crossard. The lake is well stored with brown and white trout ; and a regatta, recently held, is likely to become an annual amusement. The other seats are Elmvale, that of J. O'Brien, Esq. ; Poplar, of P. Powell, Esq. ; Inchiquin Cottage, of M. Blood, Esq., M. D. ; and Richmond, of the Rev. S. Walsh, P. P. A manorial court is occasionally held at Curofin, and petty sessions are held every alternate Wednesday. The living is a rectory and vicarage, in the diocese of Killaloe, episcopally united in 1801 to the rectory and vicarage of Kilkeedy and the vicarages of Dysert, Rath, and Inchicronane, together forming the union of Kilneboy, in the patronage of the Bishop. The tithes amount to £104. 13. ; those of the entire benefice to £469. 4. $5_{1/4}$. The glebe-house is in Kilkeedy ; the glebes comprise $28_{3/8}$ acres. The church, situated at Curofin, is a neat edifice, erected by aid of a loan of £369 from the late Board of First Fruits, in 1829 ; there is also a church in the parish of Kilkeedy. In the R. C. divisions the parish forms part of the union or district of Curofin, comprising also the parish of Rath ; there are three chapels, situated respectively at Kilneboy ; Curofin, and Rath. At Richmond is a large school under the superintendence of the R. C. clergyman, and another school is held in the chapel at Kilneboy ; in these, in the parochial school at Curofin, and in a private school, about 290 children are educated.

There are some ruins of the ancient church of Kilneboy, which appears to have been built long before the Reformation ; and near them is the base of an ancient round tower, now reduced to a height of only 12 feet, and without any aperture either for door or window. At a short distance to the north-west, and at the boundary of the lands formerly attached to the church, is a remarkable stone cross, fixed in a rock, and consisting of a shaft with two arms curving upwards ; on each of which, near the top, is a head carved in relief, and in the centre two hands clasped ; it is said to have been erected in memory of the reconciliation of two persons who had been long at violent enmity. The small village of Kilneboy is stated traditionally to have been formerly a large town, of much earlier origin than Curofin. Within a short distance from it are the ruins of a square fortress, with the remains of two angular towers, in which cannon was formerly mounted ; it is supposed to have been erected about the time of Elizabeth, is situated in low ground by the side of the river, is of difficult access, and is said to have been at one time the residence of the Deans of Kilfenora. About half a mile from the ruins of Kilneboy church are those of the church of Cood, apparently a great antiquity. Near this spot, and within the old race-course of Cood, part of the army of Jas. II. encamped in 1689. To the east of Curofin is the cemetery of the ancient church of Kilvedane, of which, though existing within the memory of many persons living, no vestige can now be traced. In this cemetery was interred Hugh Mac Curtin, a celebrated Irish antiquary, scholar, and poet ; he was author of the antiquities of Ireland, an Irish grammar, and Dictionary, and other works. At Glanquin was anciently a church, said to have been founded by St. Patrick, of which there is now no vestige, except the cemetery, which is still used ; and a Moravian church was built at Crossard, in 1793, but the society was soon dissolved and the building fell into dilapidation ; it was afterwards used as a R. C. chapel, and is now unoccupied. About two miles to the north of Kilneboy, are the remains of the ancient castle of Lemenagh, formerly the residence of the O'Brien family. On the road side, about a mile eastward from Curofin, are the beautiful and very perfect remains of the castle of Ballyportree. On the common of this parish is a very large cromlech, and there are two holy wells ; one, situated near the R. C. chapel, is surrounded with large trees, and near it are the remains of an ancient stone cross. Near Crossard is an extensive natural cavern ; and at Thaiscogh, on a rocky eminence, is a remarkable spot where seven springs have their source, and unite into one stream, which takes a subterraneous course for nearly a mile, and again emerges. Dr. Charles Lucas, a distinguished political writer on Irish affairs, is said to have been a native of this parish.

KILNEMONA, a parish, in the barony of **INCHIQUIN**, county of **CLARE**, and province of **MUNSTER**, 4 miles (W. N. W.) from Ennis, on the road to Ennistymon ; containing 1767 inhabitants. This parish, though only 3/4 of a mile in breadth, extends nearly five miles in length : it comprises 5033 statute acres, as applotted under the tithe act, about two-thirds of which are excellent arable and pasture land, and the remainder is chiefly reclaimable bog ; the state of agriculture is improving. In the eastern part is a quarry of limestone of superior quality, used for various purposes, and producing stones of considerable size which are easily detached, the strata being regularly disposed one above the other. Magowna, the residence of Ralph Cullinan, Esq., is situated near the ruins of the castle of that name, formerly the residence of Bryan O'Brien. The parish is in the diocese of Killaloe ; the rectory forms part of the rectorial union, and the vicarage part of the vicarial union, of Dromcliffe. Of the tithes, amounting to £125, three-fifths are payable to the rector and the remainder to the vicar. There is a small glebe of about one acre. In the R. C. divisions it is part of the district of Inagh, and has a chapel, which is about to be rebuilt. About 90 children are educated in a school chiefly supported by subscription. The ruins of the old church still remain in the burial-ground : at Shallee are the ruins of the castle of that name, of which no particulars are extant, and there are several ancient forts or raths.

KILNOE, a parish, in the barony of **TULLA**, county of **CLARE**, and province of **MUNSTER**, 31/2 miles (S. W.) from Scariff, on the road to Ennis ; containing 3314 inhabitants. It comprises 9940 statute acres, as applotted under the tithe act, of which 5913 consist of arable land of medium quality, and the remainder of mountain pasture and bog. The state of agriculture is likely to be much improved, in consequence of the new roads lately made in the vicinity of Lough O'Grady, a portion of which lake is within the limits of the parish. Fairs are held at Bodike on Jan. 1st, April 2nd, July 1st, and Oct. 5th ; and a court for the manor of Doonass is occasionally held at Coolreath by the seneschal, for the recovery of small debts. The seats are Coolreath, the residence of Ralph Westrop, Esq. ; St. Catherine's, of D. Sampson, Esq. ; and

Kilgorey, of M. O'Connell, Esq. The parish is in the diocese of Killaloe : part of the rectory is appropriate to the prebend of Tomgraney, and the remainder forms part of the rectorial union of Omullod ; the vicarage is part of the vicarial union of Kilseily. The tithes amount to £226. 17. 11/4., of which £33 is payable to the prebendary of Tomgraney, £92. 6. 13/4. to the rector, and the remainder to the vicar. The ruins of the old church still remain. In the R. C. divisions it forms part of the district of Tomgraney, and has a chapel at Bodike. In a school aided by the incumbent about 120, and in a private school about 220, children are educated. Near the southern shore of Lough O'Grady are the ruins of the castle of Coolreath, and of another at Ballynahince.

KILQUANE, or **ST. PATRICK'S NORTH**, a chapelry, in the barony of **BUNRATTY**, county of **CLARE**, and province of **MUNSTER**, 2 miles (N.) from Limerick, on the north side of the river Shannon ; containing 2028 inhabitants. It comprises 3719 statute acres, as applotted under the tithe act, which are chiefly in tillage : the state of agriculture has of late years considerably improved, from its proximity to the city of Limerick, of which it includes a small portion of the north liberties ; midway between Corbally mills and St. Thomas's Island is the boundary mark called the "Liberty stone." There is a considerable portion of bog; and limestone, containing fossil shells, is used for building and burnt for manure. On the river Blackwater, which runs into the Shannon, are two large flour-mills, the property of S. Caswell, Esq. Manorial courts for the recovery of small debts are occasionally held at Athlunkard and Parteen ; and at Ardnacrusha is a station of the constabulary police. The seats are Spring Hill, the residence of P. Mc Adam, Esq. ; Quinsborough, of Martin Honan, Esq. (formerly the residence of Lord George Quin); Whitehall, of Capt. R. Kane ; Fairy Hill, of E. Burnard, Esq. ; Thomas Island, of J. Tuthill, Esq. ; and Cottage, of R. Rodgers, Esq. It is a perpetual cure, forming with Singland, or St. Patrick's South, the rectory of St. Patrick, in the diocese of Limerick, and part of the union of St. Patrick and of the corps of the treasurership of the cathedral of Limerick. The tithes, amounting to £184. 12. 33/4., are payable to the rector ; the curate has a stipend of £75, and £12 per ann. from Primate Boulter's augmentation fund. The church is a neat building with a tower and spire, towards which the late Board of First Fruits granted

£700 in 1819. In the R. C. divisions it forms part of the union or district of Parteen, or Kilquane, which also includes part of the parish of Killely or Meelick, and contains the chapels of Ardnacrusha and Parteen ; the former is a handsome edifice of hewn stone. The parochial school is chiefly supported by the rector, who allows £10 per ann. and discharges the rent of the school-house ; and at Parteen is a large national school, chiefly supported by a grant of £30 per ann. from the Board. The school-house, erected by Mr. Honan in 1833, consists of a centre and two projecting wings, and contains apartments for the master and mistress. The ruins of the old church still remain in the burial-ground.

KILRAGHTIS, a parish, in the barony of **BUNRATTY**, county of **CLARE**, and province of **MUNSTER**, 3 1/2 miles (N. E.) from Ennis, on the road to Gort ; containing 1866 inhabitants. It comprises 4594 statute acres, as applotted under the tithe act, and though only one mile broad is nearly six miles long. At Ballyally is the seat of Andrew Stackpoole, Esq., and at Barefield is a very picturesque lake. The parish is in the diocese of Killaloe ; the rectory forms part of the rectorial union of Ogashin, and the vicarage part of the vicarial union of Dromcliffe. The tithes amount to £97. 7. 8 1/4., of which £46. 3. 1. is payable to the rector, and the remainder to the vicar. In the R. C. divisions it is part of the district of Dowry or Doora : there is a chapel at Barefield. The ruins of the old church still remain in the burial-ground. About 230 children are educated in three private schools.

KILRUSH, a sea-port, market and post-town, and a parish, in the barony of **MOYARTA**, county of **CLARE**, and province of **MUNSTER**, 21 miles (S. W.) from Ennis, and 130 1/4 (S. W.) from Dublin ; containing 9732 inhabitants, of which number, 3996 are in the town. This town is pleasantly situated on the northern shore of the estuary of the Shannon, about 15 miles from its mouth, and on the creek to which it gives name, and to the convenience of which for export trade it owes its present importance. It is neatly built, and consists of a market-square intersected from east to west by a spacious street, from which smaller streets branch off ; the total number of houses, in 1831, was 712, since which time several others have been added. The principal streets are well paved and flagged ; and the roads in the vicinity have been greatly improved within the last few years. The manufactures of the town and neighbourhood, chiefly for home consumption, are friezes, flannels, stockings, strong sheetings, and a serviceable kind of narrow linen, called bandle cloth. There are works for refining rock salt for domestic use, a tanyard, a soap manufactory, and a manufactory for nails. The chief trade is in corn, butter, cattle, pigs, and agricultural produce; and a considerable number of hides are sold in the market. About 20 small hookers belonging to the port are engaged in fishing and dredging for oysters off the coast, in which about 200 persons are employed. The port is free of dues, except a small charge for keeping the pier in repair. The pier, which is of very solid construction, is protected by a sea wall of great strength, and is very commodious both for commercial and agricultural uses ; it affords great facility for landing passengers from the steam-vessels which regularly ply between this place and Limerick. During the bathing season at Kilkee these vessels ply daily, and at other times only on alternate days ; public cars are always in attendance at the pier to convey passengers to Kilkee. The pier extends from the shore towards Hog island in the Shannon, and was erected partly at the expense of the Board of Customs, and subsequently extended 168 feet by the late Board of Fisheries and Mr. Vandeleur, at an expense of £1800. The custom-house, a neat modern building near the quay, erected in 1806, is under the control of the port collector of Limerick. The harbour is about 9 miles below Tarbert ; it is frequented by vessels that trade in grain and other commodities : its peculiar advantage arises from its depth of water, which admits the entrance of vessels of the largest size. Ships of war and Indiamen anchor in the roadstead, and there is a tide harbour with piers and quays ; also a patent slip for repairs. Hence it is a good asylum harbour for vessels in distress ; its proximity to the mouth of the Shannon renders it easy of access and eligible for vessels to put to sea at any time of the tide ; and therefore it must be considered the best position for an American packet station. About one mile south from the shore, and between the island of Inniscattery and the mainland, is Hog island, comprising about 20 acres of land, and containing only one family. A coast-guard station, forming part of the district of Miltown-Malbay is established at Kilrush, and a revenue cutter is stationed off the shore. Branches of the National and Agricultural banks have been opened in the town. The market is on Saturday, and by patent may be held daily ; the fairs are on May 10th, and Oct. 12th, and there is also a fair at Ballyket on July 4th. The market-house, a commodious and handsome building in the centre of the market-square, was erected at the expense of the late Mr. Vandeleur, to whom the town owes much of its prosperity ; there are also some meat shambles and a public slaughter-house. Quarter sessions are held here at Easter and Michaelmas ; petty sessions are held every Tuesday ; and a court for the manor of Kilrush is held on the first Monday in every month by the seneschal of Crofton Moore Vandeleur, Esq., lord of the manor. A chief constabulary police force is stationed in the town. The court-house, a neat and commodious building, was erected in 1831, on a site given by Mr. Vandeleur ; and a small bridewell was built in 1825, and is well adapted to the classification of prisoners.

The parish comprises 4310 statute acres, as assessed to the county rate, exclusively of a large extent of bog ; the system of agriculture has latterly. been much improved, and tillage very considerably extended ; with-in the last seven years the quantity of wheat grown has increased tenfold. This improvement is chiefly to be attributed to the facility of communication with Limerick, afforded by the steam navigation company ; the quantity of agricultural produce which passed through the market, in 1835, including pigs, amounted in value to £50,000. Great quantities of turf are cut and sent chiefly from Poolanishary harbour, on the western shore of the parish, to Limerick and its neighbourhood, by boats manned by three persons, and each boat is calculated to earn about £200 annually in this trade. At Knockeragh is an excellent quarry of flags, the smaller of which are used for roofing ; and flags of superior quality are also quarried at Moneypoint, on the shore of the Shannon, and sent to Cork, Tralee, and other places ; good grit-stones, from four to eight feet in length, and from two to four feet wide, are procured at Crag and Tullagower, with sand of a good quality for building. There are also quarries of good building stone and slate ; and in several parts of the parish are indications of lead and copper, but no mine of either has been yet explored. The principal seats are Kilrush House, the residence of Crofton Moore Vandeluer, Esq., a handsome and spacious mansion immediately adjoining the town, and commanding an extensive view of the Shannon, and the Clare and Kerry shores ; Mount Pleasant, of Capt. J. L. Cox ;

Cappa Lodge, of Randal Borough, Esq. ; and Oaklands, of W. Henn, Esq. The parish is in the diocese of Killaloe ; the rectory is partly impropriate in John Scott, Esq., but chiefly appropriate to the prebend of Inniscattery in the cathedral of Killaloe ; the vicarage also forms part of the corps of the same prebend, to which were episcopally united, in 1777, the vicarages of Kilfieragh, Kilballyhone, and Moyarta, together constituting the union of Kilrush, in the gift of the Bishop. The tithes amount to £429. 4. 7$_{1/2}$., of which £36. 18. 5$_{1/2}$. is payable to the impropriator, and the remainder to the prebendary ; and the vicarial tithes of the three other parishes amount to £365. 12. 9$_{3/4}$. The glebe-house, built by a gift of £100 and a loan of £600 from the same Board, is a handsome residence near the church ; the glebe comprises about 3 acres. The church, a large edifice with an embattled tower crowned with pinnacles, towards the erection of which the late Board of First Fruits granted a loan of £1500, was built in 1813, near the site of the ancient church, of which the ruins form an interesting and picturesque appendage : it contains a well-executed mural tablet to the late Mr. Vandeleur, and has been lately repaired by a grant of £121 from the Ecclesiastical Commissioners. In the R. C. divisions the parish is the head of a union or district, comprising also the parish of Killeymur : the parochial chapel is a spacious building, with a well-executed altar-piece ; there is also a chapel at Knockeragh, erected in 1833. There is a place of worship for Wesleyan Methodists in the town, recently erected on ground presented by Mr. Vandeleur. About 280 children are taught in three public schools, of which one is supported by the trustees of Erasmus Smith's charity, who allow the master £30 per annum ; the parochial school is chiefly supported by the incumbent, and there is a large school under the superintendence of the R. C. clergyman, who allows the master £12 per ann. : the two former are held in the upper part of the market-house, but Mr. Vandeleur has it in contemplation to build a school-house for their use. There are also four private schools, in which are about 360 children ; and a school-house has been lately built by subscription at Knockeragh. About two miles from the town, on the road to Miltown, and also near the Ennis road, are chalybeate springs, both considered efficacious in the cure of bilious diseases. At Mullagha are the ruins of an ancient chapel, supposed to have been built by St. Senan, who is said to have been a native of that place ; attached to it is a burial-ground still in use, and near it a holy well. There are several ancient forts or raths in the parish.

KILSEILY, a parish, in the barony of **TULLA**, county of **CLARE**, and province of **MUNSTER**, 9 miles (W. by S.) from Killaloe, on the road to Ennis ; containing 4227 inhabitants. It comprises 10,008 statute acres, as applotted under the tithe act ; about 7600 are good arable land under an improving system of tillage, and the remainder mountain pasture and bog. Good building-stone of a gritty quality is found in the parish ; and at Ardskegh, Hurlston, and Lyssane are quarries of slate, the produce of which is extensively used in Limerick and Ennis. The principal seats are Woodfield, that of C. Walker, Esq. ; Hurlston, of J. Bently, Esq. ; and Violet Hill, of J. Goring, Esq. Lake Doon near Broadford, abounds with pike and bream ; and the neighbourhood affords a variety of game. A canal from Broadford to Bunratty, on the Shannon, might be constructed at a moderate expense, the line being nearly level, and mostly through a chain of lakes. Two fairs are held at Broadford, *which see* ; and a manorial court for the recovery of small debts is also held there. The living is a rectory and vicarage, in the diocese of Killaloe, the rectory forming part of the union of Omullod, and the vicarage united to the vicarages of Killurane and Kilnoe, constituting the union of Kilseily, in the patronage of the Bishop. The tithes amount to £240, one-half payable to the rector and the other to the vicar ; and the entire tithes of the vicarial benefice to £313. 17. 1. The church was built at Broadford by a loan of £795 from the late Board of First Fruits, in 1811. In the R. C. divisions the parish forms part of the union or district of Broadford, comprising also the parish of Killokennedy ; there are three chapels, situated respectively at Broadford, Glanomera, and Kilbane. The parochial school at Broadford is supported by the incumbent, and there are four private schools, in which are about 330 children ; and a dispensary. There are some slight vestiges of Doon castle on the border of the lake ; and near Broadford is a mineral spring, formerly in great repute.

KILSHANNY, a parish, in the barony of **CORCOMROE**, county of **CLARE**, and province of **MUNSTER**, 2 1/4 miles (N.) from Ennistymon, on the road to Kilfenora ; containing 2013 inhabitants. Here was formerly a cell to the abbey of Corcomroe,

100

which at the dissolution was, with its appurtenances, mills, and fisheries, granted to Robert Hickman. The parish comprises 9349 statute acres, as applotted under the tithe act, and chiefly under tillage : there is a considerable portion of bog. A court for the manor of Corcomroe is occasionally held by the seneschal at Kilshanny, for the recovery of small debts. It is a rectory, in the diocese of Kilfenora, partly appropriate to the deanery, but chiefly impropriate in R. M. G. Adams, Esq. : the tithes amount to £158, of which £150 is payable to the impropriator, and the remaining £8, being the tithes of the townland of Ballymacrenan, to the dean. In the R. C. divisions this parish is held separately and gives name to the district : the chapel is at Kilshanny. In a school under the superintendence of the R. C. clergyman about 90, and in a private school about 70, children are educated. At Smithstown, a seat of Viscount Powerscourt, are the ruins of an ancient castle.

KILTONANLEA, or **DOONASS**, a parish, in the barony of **TULLA**, county of **CLARE**, and province of **MUNSTER**, 7 miles (S. S. W.) from Killaloe, on the road to Limerick, and on the river Shannon ; containing 4061 inhabitants. It comprises 6595 statute acres, as applotted under the tithe act, mostly in tillage. Limestone, in which marine shells are found imbedded, is quarried near Clonlara and chiefly burnt for manure : there is some bog. A branch of the Shannon navigation, about four miles in length, passes through this parish, to avoid the falls of Doonass between Limerick and Killaloe, and affords a daily communication by steam and other boats with those places. At Doonass are extensive bleaching establishments ; and at Clonlara are public dispensary and a station of the constabulary police. Petty sessions are held weekly on Friday at the latter place, where also a manorial court is occasionally held for the recovery of small debts ; and efforts have been recently made to re-establish the fairs usually held on March 17th, June 11th, and Sept. 21st and 29th, each continuing for two days. The seats are Doonass House, the residence of Sir Hugh Dillon Massy, Bart., beautifully situated on the Shannon ; Summer Hill, of H. Dillon Massy, Esq. ; Water Park, of S. Bindon, Esq. ; Erina House, of G. Vincent, Esq. ; Erina, of Jas. Lysaght, Esq. ; Rosehill, of P. O'Callaghan, Esq. ; Elm Hill, of Mrs. Davis ; Bellisle, of H. Mahon, Esq. ; Landscape, of P. W. Creagh, Esq. ; Springfield, of M. Gavin, Esq. ; Parkview, of Capt. Kingsmill ; Newtown, of A. Walsh, Esq. ; Mount Catherine, of G. Lloyd, Esq. ; Runnard, of Capt. J. Walsh ; and Doonass Glebe, of the Rev. T. Westrop. The living is a rectory and vicarage, in the diocese of Killaloe, episcopally united from time immemorial to the vicarage of Killokennedy, together forming the union of Kiltonanlea, or Doonass, in the patronage of the Bishop : the tithes amount to £341. 10. 9$1/4$., and the entire tithes of the benefice to £445. 5. 8$3/4$. The glebe-house was erected in 1810, when £597 was lent and £200 given by the late Board of First Fruits for that purpose : the glebe comprises 6a. 1r. 10p. The church, at Clonlara, is a neat building with a square tower surmounted by pinnacles ; for the erection of the tower and gallery the same Board granted £300, in 1831. In the R. C. divisions the parish forms part of the union or district of Doonass, which also comprises parts of the parishes of Killaloe and Killokennedy : the parochial chapel at Clonlara, erected in 1815, is a large and well-built structure ; and there is a chapel at Trugh, in the parish of Killaloe. In a school under the patronage of Lady Massy (who gives the school-house rent free), the parochial school under the superintendence of the rector, a school under that of the R. C. clergyman, and in two private schools, about 290 children are educated. Within the limits of the parish are the ruined castles of Rhinnuagh, Newtown, and Coolistigue ; and several ancient raths or forts. The "Falls of Doonass", on the Shannon, as seen from Sir H. D. Massy's demesne, have a striking and highly picturesque effect : the river, which above the falls is 300 yards wide and 40 feet deep, here pours its vast volume of water over large masses of rock extending upwards of a quarter of a mile along its course, and producing a succession of falls forming a grand and interesting spectacle.

KILTORAGHT, a parish, in the barony of **CORCOMROE**, county of **CLARE**, and province of **MUNSTER**, 3 and a half miles (W.) from Curofin, on the road from Kilfenora to Ennis; containing 1145 inhabitants. In the civil divisions it is not known as a parish, having merged into that of Kilfenora : it comprises about 3080 statute acres, as applotted under the tithe act, a large portion of which consists of mountain pasture and bog. The living is a rectory and vicarage, in the diocese of Kilfenora ; the rectory forms part of the union and corps of the deanery ; the vicarage was episcopally united, in 1795, to that of Clouney, together constituting the union of Kiltoraght in the gift of the Bishop. Of the tithes, amounting to £90, two-thirds are payable to the rector, and the remainder to the vicar. The church, for the erection of which the late Board of First Fruits gave £800, in 1813, having been injured during the late disturbances, is now in a dilapidated state ; divine service is performed at the glebe-house, for the erection of which the same Board gave £450, and lent £62, in 1814. In the R. C. divisions the parish forms part of the union or district of Kilfenora : a chapel is now being erected at Inchioveagh, on the new line of road to Ennistymon. About 110 children are educated in a private school. There are some remains of a castle at Inchioveagh.

KNOCK, a post-town, in the parish of **KILMURRY,** barony of **CLONDERALAW,** county of **CLARE**, and province of **MUNSTER**, 8 miles (W. S. W.) from Kildysart, on the road to Kilrush ; containing 180 inhabitants. It is beautifully situated on the north-western side of Clonderalaw bay, and comprises about 30 houses, several of which are ornamented in the rustic style and have tastefully disposed shrubberies and gardens attached. It is a station of the constabulary police, and petty sessions are held weekly on Friday. Here is a small pier, where sea manure is landed, and whence corn is occasionally sent in boats to Limerick.

LABASHEEDA, or **POUNDSTREET**, a village, in the parish of **KILLOFIN**, barony of **CLONDERLAW**, county of **CLARE**, and province of **MUNSTER**, 4 miles (S. W.) from Kildysert, on the lower road to Kilrush ; containing 93 houses and 466 inhabitants. From its situation on the Shannon a considerable quantity of corn is brought hither in winter, and sent in boats to Limerick ; culm obtained in the vicinity is also sent hence to Limerick, Ennis, and other places : the erection of a small pier and quay would be of great advantage to the trade. There is a ferry across the Shannon to Tarbert. A court for Lord Egremont's manor of Clonderlaw is occasionally held by the seneschal for the recovery of small debts; and a constabulary police force is stationed in the village. Near it a large R. C. chapel, a handsome cruciform building, has been lately erected.-See **KILLOFIN.**

LAHINCH, or **LAHENZY**, a village, in the parish of **KILMANAHEEN**, county of **CLARE**, and province of **MUNSTER**, 2 miles (W.) from Ennistymon, on the bay of Liscannor, on the western coast ; containing 195 houses and 1033 inhabitants. This place has of late rapidly improved on account of its fine bathing strand, situated at the inner extremity of the bay, and much resorted to during the season. The roads in the vicinity have been greatly improved, and when the new bridge over the estuary of the river Inagh between this place and Liscanor shall be completed, there will be an uninterrupted drive along the coast from Miltown-Malbay to the cliffs of Moher. The village affords good accommodation for visiters, and races are generally held every season for their amusement. In the vicinity are the natural curiosities called the "Puffing Holes" and the "Dropping Well; " the former is described under the head of Miltown-Malbay ; the latter is similar to the dropping well at Knaresborough, in Yorkshire : the surrounding scenery is extremely picturesque and diversified. In the village is the R. C. chapel for this portion of the district of Ennistymon, in which a school is held under the superintendence of the parish priest.

LISCANOR, a village, in the parish of **KILMACREHY**, barony of **CORCOMROE**, county of **CLARE**, and province of **MUNSTER**, 4 miles (W.) from Ennistymon, on the northern side of the bay of the same name on the western coast ; containing 77 houses and 506 inhabitants. The bay being exposed to the violence of the Atlantic, and having a rocky and dangerous shore, a pier was built at this place a few years since, by the late Fishery Board, for the protection and encouragement of the small craft employed in the fishery of the bay, to which, as well as to vessels engaged in general trading, it affords great shelter and accommodation, although it has been several times injured by the sea. Excellent lobsters, small turbot, and a variety of other fish are taken in the bay. Here are a constabulary police station, and a detachment from the coast-guard station at Freagh Point. Over the estuary of the river Inagh, in the vicinity of the village, a handsome bridge is now in course of erection, consisting of three elliptic arches, each of 45 feet span, connected by a causeway or embankment, 160 feet in length, with three smaller arches on the south side for the passage of superfluous water ; the total length of the roadway, including an embankment at each end of the bridge, is 507 feet.

Of the estimated expense, £4200, the Board of Public Works, under whose superintendence it is being erected, has contributed £2222 ; the remainder being defrayed by the county. In the R. C. divisions, this village gives name to a district, which comprises the parishes of Kilmacrehy and Killaspuglenane, and contains the chapels of Liscanor in the former and Cahirgal in the latter parish: that of Liscanor is a large plain building. Near the village are the ruins of an ancient castle, consisting of a large square tower : it was formerly of great strength, and was the residence of the O'Conors.-See **KILMACREHY.**

LISDEEN, a village, in the parish of **KILFIERAGH**, barony of **MOYARTA**, county of **CLARE**, and province of **MUNSTER**, 2 miles (E.) from Kilkee, near the road from that place to Kilrush ; containing 7 houses and 45 inhabitants. The population has considerably decreased since the increase of buildings at Kilkee. Fairs are held on May 7th, July 13th, Sept. 8th, and Dec. 17th. Here is the old R. C. chapel for the parish of Kilfieragh ; and in the vicinity is a chalybeate spring, occasionally used for medicinal purposes.

LISDOONVARNA, county of CLARE.-See **KILMOON.**

LOUGHRASK, a hamlet, in the parish of **DROMCREEHY**, barony of **BURREN**, county of **CLARE**, and province of **MUNSTER** ; containing 17 houses and 95 inhabitants.

MEELICK, county of CLARE.-See **KILLELY.**

MILTOWN-MALBAY, a post-town, in the parish of **KILFARBOY**, barony of **IBRICKANE**, county of **CLARE**, and province of **MUNSTER**, 23 miles (W.) from Ennis (by Ennistymon), and 134$_{1/2}$ (W. S. W.) from Dublin, by way of Limerick ; containing 133 houses and 726 inhabitants. It is situated near the western coast, and contiguous to the great recess which, from its dangerous shore, is called the Malbay. Owing to the exertions of the late Mr. Morony, this place, since the commencement of the present century, has risen from a mere hamlet to be a fashionable bathing-place ; and among the houses, which are in general neatly built, are several of a superior description, occupied as bathing-lodges during the season. Near Spanish Point (so called from part of the Spanish Armada having been wrecked there in the reign of Queen Elizabeth) is the hotel, forming with its out-offices a handsome and extensive range of building. It was erected, in 1810, by a company, consisting of the Morony family and other gentlemen, and, besides the usual accommodations of an hotel, contains hot and cold baths, billiard-rooms, and a spacious assembly-room ; it commands extensive views of the Atlantic, and adjoins the bathing strand, which is considered one of the best on the western coast : attached is stabling for nearly sixty horses. Though devoid of wood, the fine sea views, the elevation of the land and the dryness of the soil, together with the excellent roads in the vicinity, combine to render this place agreeable ; and it is in consequence frequented during the bathing season by fashionable visiters from various parts of the country, for whose amusement races are occasionally held. Fairs are held on Feb. 1st, March 9th, May 4th, June 20th, Aug. 11th, Oct. 18th, and Dec. 9th, for general farming stock. Quarter sessions are held here in June ; petty sessions weekly on Thursday ; and a court for Lord Egremont's manor of Moih Ibrickane monthly, for the recovery of small debts : near the town is a station of the constabulary police. Here are the parish church and the R. C. chapel of the district, which, together with the seats in the vicinity, are noticed under the head of Kilfarboy. At Freagh, on the coast, is a natural curiosity called the "Puffing Hole," which spouts water with great force to a considerable height, and when the sun shines forms at each emission a beautiful iris. At Cassino, in the vicinity, is a chalybeate spa.

MOHER CLIFFS.-See **KILMACREHY.**

MOUNT-SHANNON, a village, in that part of the parish of **INNISCALTHRA** which is in the barony of **LEITRIM,** county of **GALWAY,** and province of **CONNAUGHT,** 7³/₄ miles (N. by W.) from Killaloe, on the road from Woodford to Limerick ; containing 171 inhabitants. This place is beautifully situated on Lough Deirgeart, on the confines of the county and province. Here and at Knockafort are piers, where vessels of 20 tons' burden can load and unload. It is a constabulary police station ; and petty sessions are held here. There is a market-house ; fairs are held on the 28th of Feb., May, Aug., and Nov. ; and a patent exists for a monthly fair, which is not held. It contains the parish church, and a R.C. chapel, erected in 1836.-See **INNISCALTHRA**.

MOYARTA, or **MOYFERTA**, a parish, in the barony of **MOYARTA**, county of **CLARE**, and province of **MUNSTER**, 9 miles (S. W.) from Kilrush, on the western coast ; containing 7441 inhabitants. It forms part of a peninsula bounded on the north-west by the Atlantic, and on the south-east by the river Shannon, and comprises 7967 statute acres, as rated for the county cess, the greater part of which is under tillage ; sea-weed and sand are extensively used for manure, and the state of agriculture is gradually improving : loose limestone is found in the cliffs on that part of the coast called the White Strand. Within the limits of the parish are the bay of Carrigaholt (noticed in the article on that place), the creek of Querin, and part of an inlet called Scagh or Poulanishery, all on the Shannon side of the peninsula. Querin creek produces fine shrimps and flat fish, and affords a safe harbour for boats that fit out here for the herring fishery. The inlet of Poulanishery, which extends three miles inland in two different directions, also affords safe anchorage for small vessels : a vast quantity of turf is annually sent hence to Limerick and other places, and at its mouth is a ferry, communication between Kilrush parish and "the West", as this peninsula is generally called. To distinguish by night the proper course on entering the Shannon, a light has been established on the summit of Kilkadrane Hill, red sea-ward, with a bright fixed light towards the river. At Kilkadrane is a station of the coast-guard, being one of the six constituting the district of Miltown-Malbay. At Querin is the residence of Lieut. Borough, R. N., a curious building in the old Dutch style, with a long projecting roof, which, together with the bricks, is said to have been made in Holland for Mr. Vanhoogart, who built the house ; at Dunaha is the ancient residence of the Moroney family ; and at Mount Pleasant is the residence of Joseph Cox, Esq. The parish is in the diocese of Killaloe ; part of the rectory is impropriate in the Representatives of Lord Castlecoote, and the remainder forms part of the corps of the prebend of Inniscattery ; the vicarage forms part of the union of Kilrush. The tithes amount to £470. 15. 4$\frac{3}{4}$., of which £208. 18. 5$\frac{3}{4}$. is payable to the impropriator, and the remainder to the incumbent, as prebendary and vicar. In the R. C. divisions it forms part of the union or district of Dunaha, also called

Carrigaholt, comprising the parishes of Moyarta and Kilballyhone, and containing the chapels of Dunaha, Carrigaholt, and Cross : that of Carrigaholt is a modern edifice. At Clarefield is a school, established by, and under the patronage of, Joseph Cox, Esq., aided by subscription. The ruins of the old church still remain, and the burial-ground contains some tombstones inscribed with the celebrated French name Conti, some of whom are supposed to have been visiters of the Clare family, at the neighbouring castle of Carrigaholt. On a small spot containing about an acre of land, nearly insulated by the Atlantic, are the remains of Dunlicky Castle, the approach to which is guarded by a high and narrow tower with a wall on each side ; at Knocknagarron are the remains of an old signal tower, or telegraph ; and at Carrigaholt are those of the castle called Carrick-an-oultagh, or "the Ulsterman's rock," said to have been built by a native of the county of Down, and once the residence of the ancient family of Mac Mahon.-See **CARRIGAHOLT**.

MOYNOE, a parish, in the barony of **TULLA**, county of **CLARE**, and province of **MUNSTER,** 8 miles (N. N. W.) from Killaloe ; containing 1268 inhabitants. It is situated on the confines of the county of Galway, and extends to within a mile of the town of Scariff ; comprising about 1940 statute acres of arable land in a tolerable state of cultivation, exclusively of a large portion of coarse mountain pasture and bog. The only seat is Moynoe House, the residence of Fitzgibbon Hinchy, Esq. It is in the diocese of Killaloe ; the rectory is appropriate to the economy fund of the cathedral of Killaloe, and the vicarage forms part of the union of Inniscalthra : the tithes amount to £83. 1. 6½., of which £46. 3. 1. is payable to the economy fund, and the remainder to the vicar. In the R. C. divisions it is part of the union or district of Scariff. The ruins of the old church still remain.

MULLOGH, a hamlet, in the parish of **KILMURRY**, barony of **IBRICKANE**, county of **CLARE**, and province of **MUNSTER** ; containing 17 houses and 96 inhabitants. Here is a R. C. chapel, belonging to the district of Milltown.

MUNCHIN (ST.), a parish, partly in the barony of **BUNRATTY**, county of **CLARE**, but chiefly in the North liberties of the city of

LIMERICK, and province of **MUNSTER**, on the river Shannon, and immediately adjoining the city ; containing 3883 inhabitants. This parish, which is divided into two parts by the intervening parishes of St. Nicholas and Killeely, comprises 3633 statute acres of arable and pasture land, exclusively of about 640 acres of waste and bog : excellent building stone is found within its limits. That portion of the city which stands on King's Island is chiefly in this parish, and is connected with the North liberties by the ancient bridge of Thomond, now about to be taken down and rebuilt by the Board of Public Works. The seats are Castle Park, the residence of C. Delmege, Esq. ; Ballygrennan, of Rich. Smyth, Esq. ; and Clonmacken, the property of the Marquess of Lansdowne, at present unoccupied. It is in contemplation to erect several respectable residences at Kilrush, in the North liberties, in consequence of the facility of communication with the city recently afforded by the erection of Wellesley bridge. The living is a rectory and vicarage, in the diocese of Limerick, united to the rectory and vicarage, of Killelonehan and rectory of Drehidtarsna, together constituting the corps of the prebend of St. Munchin in the cathedral of Limerick, and in the gift of the bishop : the tithes amount to £276. 18. 6$\frac{1}{2}$., and the gross value of the prebend is £455. 13. 8. There is a glebe-house, with a glebe of 5 acres, but the former has been condemned by the Ecclesiastical Commissioners. The church stands near Thomond bridge, on the southern bank of the Shannon : it was erected in 1827, nearly on the site of the ancient edifice, which is said to have been built so early as the year 561, and to have been once the cathedral of the diocese. Tradition states that it was burnt by the Danes, in apparent confirmation of which a stratum of ashes was found on removing the foundation in 1827. The present church is a neat structure with a square tower surmounted by pinnacles, erected at an expense of about £1400, of which £900 was a loan from the late Board of First Fruits, and the remainder was defrayed by subscription. A fine view of the Shannon is obtained from the churchyard. In the R. C. divisions the parish is partly in the union or district of Thomond Gate, comprising also parts of St. Nicholas and Killeely, and containing the chapel of St. Lelia near Thomond Gate, a substantial and spacious building, erected in 1798 ; and a small chapel at Woodthorpe : the remainder of St. Munchin's parish is in the Limerick district. On King's island are the remains of an ancient Dominican friary, near which a nunnery has been established : attached is a large school for girls, who are gratuitously instructed by the ladies of the convent. Near the church is a range of almshouses and schools, endowed by Mrs. Hannah Villiers, and erected by her trustees in 1826. The building, which is in the Elizabethan style, consists of a centre and two projecting wings, the former being surmounted by a cupola : it contains apartments for 12 poor widows, each of whom receives £24 Irish per annum ; and there are two school-rooms. The master receives £30, and the mistress £25, per annum. Under a recent decree in chancery the trustees are about to establish a Protestant female orphan school, for the maintenance and education of 20 poor children. Near the north end of Thomond bridge is an ancient stone on which it is said the treaty of Limerick was signed : it is still called the "treaty stone." The churchyard is supposed to have been the burial-place of St. Munchin, the first Bishop of Limerick ; the church contains a monument to Bishop Smyth, who lived, died, and was buried in this parish, and it is the burial-place of the family of Smyth, ennobled in the person of the present Lord Gort.

MURROGHTWOHY, a village, in the parish of **GLANINAGH**, barony of **BURREN**, county of **CLARE**, and province of **MUNSTER** ; containing 35 houses and 212 inhabitants.

MUTTON ISLAND, county of CLARE.-See **ENNISKERRY.**

NAUGHAVAL.-See **NOUGHAVAL**.

NEWMARKET-ON-FERGUS, a post-town in the parish of **TOMFINLOE**, barony of **BUNRATTY**, county of **CLARE**, and province of **MUNSTER**, 6 miles (S. E. by E.) from Ennis, on the mail road to Limerick, and 105 1/4 (W. S. W.) from Dublin; containing 1118 inhabitants. It is situated about a mile and a half from the eastern shore of the river Fergus, and in 1831 contained 170 houses, several of which are neatly built. A market was formerly held here on Thursday, but from its proximity to Ennis and Limerick, to which places there are several daily public conveyances, it gradually declined and is now discontinued ; and of the fairs, held on March 31st, Aug. 27th, and Dec. 20th, the last only is now well attended : a "patron" is held on Easter-Monday.

Here is a chief station of the constabulary police ; petty sessions are held on alternate Thursdays, and a court for Lord Egremont's manor of Bunratty is occasionally held by the seneschal, for the recovery of small debts. A considerable number of females are employed in satin-stitching on muslin by Wm. Lloyd, Esq., of Limerick : and a school for embroidery is patronized by Lady O'Brien. An unsuccessful attempt was some time since made by Sir Edw. O'Brien to establish the linen manufacture in this town. Newmarket gives name to the R. C. union or district, held by the administrator of the Bishop of Killaloe, and comprising the parishes of Tomfinloe, Kilnasoolagh, Kilmaleery, Clonloghan, Kilconry, Bunratty, and Dromline. The principal chapel, a spacious and substantial building, is in the town ; and there are chapels for the rural district at Kilmaleery and Bunratty. A large national school-house is now being erected at the expense of Sir Edward O'Brien, by whom also it will be chiefly supported ; and a female school of industry is supported by a society of ladies : there is also a dispensary. Newmarket House, the spacious mansion of C. Studdert, Esq., is in the town ; and in its vicinity are several handsome seats, among which are Dromoland, the superb castellated edifice of Sir Edward O'Brien, Bart. ; Carrigoran, the beautifully situated mansion of Sir Wm. Fitzgerald, Bart. ; Glenwood, the residence of Basil Davoren, Esq.; Ballykilty, of Fitzgerald Blood, Esq. ; and Mogullane, of F. Healy, Esq.-See **TOMFINLOE.**

NEW-QUAY, county of CLARE.-See **ABBEY.**

NOUGHAVAL, a parish, in the barony of **BURREN**, county of **CLARE**, and province of **MUNSTER**, 2 miles (N. N. E.) from Kilfenora, on the road from Ennis to Burren ; containing 408 inhabitants, of which number, 64 are in the hamlet. It comprises 4521 statute acres, as applotted under the tithe act, only a small portion of which is under tillage, the greater part consisting of rocky limestone pasture, yielding a rich though scanty herbage : there are about 80 acres of pasturable mountain. The living is a rectory and vicarage, in the diocese of Kilfenora, united at a period unknown to the vicarage of Carrune, or Carne, together constituting the union of Noughaval and the corps of the precentorship of Kilfenora, in the patronage of the Bishop. The tithes amount to £35, and of the entire benefice to £70, the whole payable to the Ecclesiastical Commissioners, by whom the benefice is at present held in sequestration : the glebe comprises 26*a*. 0*r*. 22*p*. In the R. C. divisions the parish forms part of the union or district of Carrune, or Carne : the chapel is at the village of Noughaval. About 35 children are educated in a private school. The ruins of the church stand on the glebe : and at Banroe, Ballymurphy, and Ballygannor are the ruins of the castles respectively so called. Within the limits of the parish are three ancient forts, attributed to the Danes ; and at Ballygannor is a cromlech of extraordinary dimensions, the table stone being nearly 40 feet long and 10 broad, and supported by upright flag stones, rising about six feet above the ground.

O'BRIEN'S-BRIDGE, a village, in the parish of **KILLALOE**, barony of **TULLA**, county of **CLARE**, and province of **MUNSTER**, 6 miles (S. W.) from Limerick, on the road to Killaloe; containing 350 inhabitants. This place, which is situated on the Shannon, derives its name from a bridge of 14 arches built over that river by one of the O'Briens, which for several centuries has withstood the violent impetuosity of the current. The arches vary in span from 19 to 28 feet, and four of them at the north end have been taken down by the Government engineers, who have replaced them by two cast-iron arches, each 60 feet span, and dredged the river to the depth of 7 feet. The village consists of one street and contains about 60 houses neatly built ; the neighbourhood is embellished with several handsome seats, of which the principal are Clonboy, the residence of J. Brown, Esq. ; Ross, of T. Westropp, Esq. ; the residence of Major Boucher, on the margin of the Shannon ; Fuhers Lodge, of M. Garvin, Esq. ; and Fairy Lawn, of Capt. Twiss. An extensive flour and oatmeal mill, worked by steam, the property of Messrs. Hood and Boyd, late of Glasgow, affords employment to 50 men. Fairs are held on July 25th and Nov. 7th, and packet boats pass daily to Dublin and Limerick. Near the village is Montpelier, a strongly impregnated sulphureous spring, in high repute for its efficacy in cutaneous diseases, and much frequented. A church was erected here in 1822, for which purpose the late Board of First Fruits made a free grant of £300. The living is a perpetual curacy, in the diocese of Killaloe, and in the patronage of the Dean and Chapter ; the stipend is £75, payable by the Bishop ; a glebe-house has been built at Ross, on a site presented by Thomas Westropp, Esq., who also gave 6 acres of glebe.

OGASHIN.-See **QUINN.**

OGONNILLOE, a parish, in the barony of **TULLA**, county of **CLARE**, and province of **MUNSTER**, 5 miles (N. by W.) from Killaloe, on the road to Scariff ; containing 2966 inhabitants. It is situated on the southern side of Scariff bay, which opens into Lough Derg, and comprises 5554 statute acres, including the island of Coskerry, in Lough Derg, which contains 157 acres. The whole of the parish, with the exception only of about 97 acres, is the property of Major Purdon. The land is partly in pasture, but chiefly in tillage, and there is some mountain bog. An excellent new road has been lately constructed along the shores of Lough Derg, by which the hilly road from Scariff to Killaloe, through the centre of the parish, is avoided. Petty sessions are held generally on alternate Mondays at Annacarriga. The more elevated parts, and in particular the Gap of Ogonnilloe, command fine views of the lough, the Derry hills on the opposite shore, and the Keeper mountain in the distance. Tinerana, the residence of Major Purdon, is beautifully situated on the banks of Lough Derg, in an extensive and well-wooded demesne. The living is a vicarage, in the diocese of Killaloe, and in the gift of the Bishop ; the rectory is partly appropriate to the economy fund of the cathedral of Killaloe, and the remainder forms part of the union of Omullod : the tithes amount to £175. 7. 8$_{1/4}$., of which £38. 15. 4$_{1/2}$. is payable to the economy fund, £78. 9. 2$_{3/4}$. to the incumbent of Omullod, and the remainder to the vicar, who also receives £34. 6. from the economy fund. The glebe-house was built in 1814, when the late Board of First Fruits contributed a gift of £450, and a loan of £63, towards its erection : attached is a glebe comprising about 10 acres. The church is a neat edifice, with a tower surmounted by minarets, erected in 1810, by aid of a gift of £800 from the same Board. In the R. C. divisions the parish forms a separate district : the chapel is at the Gap of Ogonnilloe. About 70 children are educated in a school at Tinerana, under the superintendence of the vicar, and supported by subscription ; the school-house was built by Mr. Purdon. A Sunday school is superintended by Miss Purdon, and about 230 children are educated in three private schools. At Ballybran are the ruins of an old church, and on a small island about 100 yards from the shore are the remains of Cahir castle. Until lately this castle was almost perfect, but having been used for illicit distillation, it was partly blown up a few years since, and now forms a picturesque ruin.

OMULLOD.-See **CLONLEA.**

OUGHTMANNA, or **OUGHTMAMA**, a parish, in the barony of **BURREN**, county of **CLARE**, and province of **MUNSTER**, 4 miles (S.) from Burren : containing 793 inhabitants. It is chiefly situated on the confines of the county of Galway, but two detached portions, forming the headlands called respectively Aughnish point and Finvarra point, are situated on Galway bay : on each of these points is a Martello tower. The parish comprises 9558 statute acres, as applotted under the tithe act, a large portion of which consists of rocky mountain pasture : sea weed is in general use for manuring the parts in tillage. It is a rectory and vicarage, in the diocese of Kilfenora, forming part of the union of Kilcorney and of the corps of the chancellorship of Kilfenora ; the tithes amount to £120. In the R. C. divisions it is part of the union or district of Abbey. About 120 children are taught in a school under the superintendence of the R. C. clergyman. On the border of a lough, in this parish, are the ruins of Turlough Castle, of which no account is extant.

QUIN, a parish, in the barony of **BUNRATTY**, county of **CLARE**, and province of **MUNSTER**, 5 1/2 miles (S. E.) from Ennis, on the old road to Limerick ; containing 2918 inhabitants, of which number 173 are in the village. It was anciently called Quint or Quinchy, where, about 1250, an abbey was founded, which was consumed by fire in 1278. About the commencement of the 15th century, according to the Annals of the Four Masters, a monastery for Franciscan friars of the Strict Observance was founded here by Sioda Cam Macnamara, which is said to have been the first house of the Franciscan order in Ireland that admitted this reformation. The buildings, of which the remains still exist, were erected chiefly of a kind of black marble by Macon Dall Macnamara, Lord of Glancoilean, whose tomb still remains. The monastery with all its possessions was granted, in 1583, to Sir Turlogh O'Brien, of Ennistymon, and in 1604 the buildings were repaired. In the vicinity, Teigue O'Brien, son of Sir Turlogh, who had revolted from the English government, was defeated in 1601 by Capt. Flower and mortally wounded. The village, which in 1831 contained 34 houses, is a station of the constabulary police and has a penny post to Newmarket-on-Fergus. Fairs are held on July 7th, and Nov. 1st, and petty sessions on alternate Wednesdays. The parish comprises 7290 statute acres, as applotted under the tithe act, of which 5190 only are rated for the county cess ; the land is chiefly in tillage, but there is a considerable portion of rocky land, affording a scanty though rich pasturage, and about 320 acres of bog : although there is an abundance of limestone adapted both for building and agricultural purposes, and a good supply of sea manure brought up the river Fergus, the state of agriculture is rather backward. The Quin river, which flows into the Fergus, abounds with fine eels. At Ballyhickey is a productive lead mine, the property of Hugh Singleton, Esq., worked by a mining company ; the ore, which is of superior quality, is conveyed to Clare, where it is shipped for Wales. The seats are Moriesk, the finely wooded demesne of Lord Fitzgerald and Vesci ; Well Park, of the Rt. Rev. Dr. Mac Mahon, R. C. bishop of Killaloe ; Quinville Abbey, the handsome mansion of John Singleton, Esq., recently rebuilt in the Elizabethan style ; Knopouge Castle, the residence of Wm. Scott, Esq., which formerly belonged to the Macnamaras of Moriesk, and is one of the few ancient castles still inhabited ; Castle Fergus, the modern residence of Wm. Smith, Esq., adjoining which are the remains of the ancient edifice ; Ballykilty, the residence of John Blood Esq. ; Dangan, the property of Rich. Creagh, Esq. ; and Lough O'Connell, of Thos. Steele, Esq. From a turret on the summit of Mount Cullane, in Mr. Steele's demesne, is obtained an extensive and interesting view of the surrounding country, embracing a number of lakes, of which that called "Lough O'Connell" lies immediately at its base.

The living is a rectory and vicarage, in the diocese of Killaloe ; the rectory is united to those of Cloney, Dowry, Kilraghtis, Templemaly, Kilmurrynegaul, and the half-rectory of Tullagh, together constituting the union of Ogashin, in the patronage of the Earl of Egremont ; the vicarage is episcopally united to those of Cloney and Dowry, together forming the union of Quin, in the gift of the Bishop. The tithes amount to £175. 7. 8$\frac{1}{2}$., of which £71. 1. 6$\frac{1}{2}$. is payable to the rector, £81. 4. 7$\frac{1}{2}$. to the vicar, and the remaining £23. 1. 61/2. to the prebendary of Tullagh : the gross tithes of the rectorial union amount to £495. 13. 101/4, and of the vicarial union to £279. 13. 101/4. The glebe-house, towards the erection of which the late Board of First Fruits, in 1822, granted £450 as a gift and £200 as a loan, is a commodious residence ; the glebe of union comprises 15 acres. The church is a small plain building with a low tower, erected in 1797, by aid of a gift of £500 from the late Board ; and the Ecclesiastical Commissioners have lately granted £100 for its repair. In the R. C. divisions the parish is the head of a union or district, comprising also the parish of Cloney, each containing a chapel. A new chapel is now in course of erection at Quin ; it is a handsome and spacious cruciform structure, in the Gothic style, with a portico of hewn stone ; the estimated expense, £2000, is being defrayed by subscription. About 130 children are educated in two private schools. At the village is a dispensary. Quin abbey is considered to be one of the finest and most complete remains of monastic antiquity in Ireland: it is situated on a gentle slope near a small stream, having an ascent of several steps to the church, which consists of a nave and chancel, with a tower in the centre, and a chapel on the south side of the altar. In the chapel is a rudely sculptured figure in relief of some saint, and in the chancel is the monument of the founder's family. The cloisters are adorned with coupled pillars and ornamental buttresses, and on three sides of them extend respectively the refectory, dormitory, and a grand room to the north of the chancel, under all of which are vaulted rooms. To the north of the large room is a private way to a strong tower, the walls of which are nearly ten feet thick ; and adjoining the abbey are the remains of a building supposed to have been appropriated to the accommodation of strangers. The south end of the abbey is of much superior workmanship to the adjoining parts, but the whole is much disfigured by the custom of burying within the walls. Besides the castles of Knopouge and Fergus before mentioned, there are the remains of the castles of Ballymarkahan, Dangan, and Danganbrack. Dangan castle is said to be one of the oldest in Munster, having been built by Philip de Clare, from whom the county of Thomond has since been called Clare. It was with other possessions granted by Chas. II. to Pierse Creagh for his services against Cromwell, and still remains in the possession of the descendants of the original grantee. It was formerly a place of some strength, and was of a quadrangular form, flanked at each angle by a small round tower : from the centre rose the donjon or keep. The ruins form a picturesque object in the well-planted demesne of Dangan. The castle of Danganbrack is now in the Scott family, having, with Knopouge, been purchased from the Macnamaras, as Moriesk has more recently been by the father of Lord Fitzgerald and Vesci.

RATH, a parish, in the barony of **INCHIQUIN**, county of **CLARE**, and province of **MUNSTER**, 53/4 miles (N. W.) from Ennis, on the road to Ennistymon ; containing 2521 inhabitants. It comprises about 5000 statute acres, as rated for the county cess, which estimate was taken as the basis for the tithe composition ; a considerable portion consists of coarse pasture, and the remainder of good arable land. The parish extends to the bridge at Corofin, and comprises portions of the lakes of Inchiquin and Tadane, noticed in the article on Kilneboy : at Riverston is a chief station of the constabulary police. The seats are Adephi, the residence of F. and W. Fitzgerald, Esqrs. ; Clifden, of E. Burton, Esq. ; Roxton, of T. Blood, Esq. ; Applevale, of G. Davis, Esq. ; Willbrook, of W.A. Brewe, Esq. ; and Riverston, of Jonas Studdert, Esq. The living is a rectory and vicarage, in the diocese of Killaloe ; the rectory was united in 1803 to that of Dysert, together constituting the corps of the prebend of Rath, in the patronage of the Marquess of Thomond ; and the vicarage forms part of the union and corps of the prebend of Dysert. Of the tithes, amounting to £76. 15. 01/2., two-thirds are payable to the prebendary, and the remainder to the vicar. In the R. C. divisions the parish forms part of the union or district of Corofin ; the chapel, a small plain building, is at Liscullane. About 30 children are taught in a school at Knockmacart, chiefly supported by Mr. Blood and Mr. Synge, and about 70 in a school held in the chapel. The ruins of the ancient church stand near a margin of a small lake ; near them are those of the castle of Rath, and in the vicinity, those of a castle called O'Nial's Court, formerly the residence of the chieftains of that family. A large monumental stone near the castle records its destruction, and that of part of the family, by lightning. The ruins of Tier Mac Bran castle are situated near the shore of Inchiquin lake.

RATHBOURNEY, a parish, in the barony of **BURREN**, county of **CLARE,** and province of **MUNSTER**, 81/2 miles (W. S .W.)

from Burren, on the road to Ennistymon ; containing 848 inhabitants. It comprises 9440 statute acres, as applotted under the tithe act, a large portion of which consists of rocky mountain pasture, affording a rich though scanty herbage : there is also a portion of bog. The principal residence is Gregans, that of Fras. Martin, Esq. It is a rectory and vicarage, in the diocese of Kilfenora, forming part of the union of Dromcrehy and corps of the treasurership of Kilfenora : the tithes amount to £100. The church of the union, a small plain building without a tower, erected about 40 years since, is within the limits of the parish. In the R. C. divisions it is the head of the union or district of Glyn or Glenarragha, comprising also the parishes of Dromcrehy, Glaninagh, and Killonoghan. The chapel at Glenarragha was originally built by the late Marquess of Buckingham, and has been recently much enlarged. A glebe of 40 acres is allotted for the use of the parish priest, subject to a rent of £20 per annum ; about 60 children are educated in a private school. At Gregans, on the border of the parish, are the ruins of the castle of that name.

RUAN, county of CLARE.-See **DYSERT.**

SCARIFF, a post-town, in the parish of **TOMGRANEY**, barony of **TULLA**, county of **CLARE**, and province of **MUNSTER**, 8 miles (N. W. by N.) from Killaloe and 94 3/4 (W. by S.) from Dublin, on the road from Killaloe to Williamstown and Portumna; containing 761 inhabitants. It is situated on the river Scariff, which flows into the picturesque bay of the same name, opening into Lough Derg on the Shannon, and might be easily made navigable from the bay to Lough Grady, about a mile above the town : the river is here crossed by a bridge of three arches. This is a pleasing little town, occupying an ascent from the river, and consisting chiefly of one main street : in 1831 it contained 120 houses, some of which are neatly built. An excellent new and level road, which has been lately constructed between Killaloe and Williamstown, chiefly along the shores of Lough Derg, passes through the town. Here are extensive oil and flour-mills, and a considerable number of coarse hats are manufactured in the immediate vicinity. Fairs are held monthly. A smelting furnace for iron was formerly in full work here. In the R. C. divisions it gives name to a union or district, comprising the north-eastern part of the parish of Tomgraney, and the entire parish of Moynoe, and containing the chapels of Scariff and Knock O'Grady. During the disturbances, in 1831, an encampment was formed on Shene hill, in the vicinity, which was occupied for two months by a party of the military.

SIX-MILE-BRIDGE, a post-town, partly in the parish of **KILFENTINAN**, barony of **BUNRATTY**, but chiefly in that of **KILFINAGHTY**, barony of **TULLA**, county of **CLARE**, and province of **MUNSTER**, 8 miles (N. W. by W.) from Limerick, and 101¾ (W. S. W.) from Dublin, on the old mail road from Limerick to Ennis ; containing 1491 inhabitants. This place is called in Irish *Abhuinn O'Gearna*, from the river Gearna or Ougarnee, on which it is situated : it was formerly of some note, and had a chapel or vicarial house belonging to the Dominican friars of St. Saviour, Limerick, of which no vestige now exists. The town, which is irregularly built, in 1831 contained 229 houses: although advantageously situated on the river Ougarnee, which flows into the Shannon at Bunratty, and is navigable thence for boats to within half a mile of the town, it has been long declining ; its market, formerly held on Friday, is discontinued, and the market-house, once a handsome building, is now unroofed. A large mill, formerly used for grinding corn, and since used as a paper-mill, has lately been discontinued ; as have some mills below the town for several years. A fair held on Dec. 5th for store and fat cattle is much frequented by provision merchants from Cork and Limerick. General sessions are held here in June ; petty sessions occasionally on Tuesdays ; and a seneschal's court usually once in six weeks, for the recovery of small debts. A constabulary police force is stationed in the town. The sessions-house is a commodious building, attached to which is a small but well regulated bridewell. Here are the church of the union of Bunratty, and the principal R. C. chapel of the district. The former is an old edifice, of which the tower, being considered insecure, was taken down a few years since, and for rebuilding it and repairing the church the Ecclesiastical Commissioners have lately granted £542. In the R. C. divisions Six-mile-bridge gives name to the union or district, comprising the parishes of Kilmurrynegaul, Kilfinaghty, and Finogh, and containing the chapels of Six-mile-bridge and Kilmurry ; the former is a spacious modern building. The school-house near the chapel is a large building, erected by subscription about 10 years since ; the classics are taught in this school, which is under the superintendence of the parish priest. A dispensary for the poor is open three days in the week.

TEMPLEMALY, a parish, in the barony of **BUNRATTY**, county of **CLARE**, and province of **MUNSTER**, 3 1/2 miles (N.) from Ennis, near the road to Corofin ; containing 1554 inhabitants. This parish, which, though only about one mile broad, is nearly five miles long, comprises 3781 statute acres, as applotted under the tithe act : within its limits are several lakes, and about 100 acres of bog ; one of the lakes, which abounds with fish and contains a small island, is supposed to have a subterraneous communication with another lake, about a mile and half distant. It is a rectory and vicarage in the diocese of Killaloe ; the rectory forming part of the rectorial union of Ogashin, and the vicarage part of the vicarial union of Dromcliffe. The tithes amount to £105. 16. 9., of which £49. 16. 11. is payable to the rector, and the remainder to the vicar. There is a small glebe of about one acre. In the R. C. divisions it is part of the union or district of Dowry, or Doora. About 60 children are educated in a school held in a house given rent-free by Mrs. Craven. The ruins of the ancient church still exist.

TOMFINLOE, or **TOMFINLOGH**, a parish, in the barony of **BUNRATTY**, county of **CLARE**, and province of **MUNSTER**, 4 miles (N. W.) from Six-mile-bridge, on the road to Ennis ; containing, with the town of Newmarket-on-Fergus, 4053 inhabitants. It comprises 3424 statute acres, as applotted under the tithe act : the land is in general rich, and chiefly in pasture ; there is, however, some craggy land and bog : the state of agriculture has been much improved, chiefly owing to the example and exertions of Sir Edward O'Brien of Dromoland, Bart. Fairs and petty sessions are held at Newmarket, *which see*. Besides the seats noticed under the head of Newmarket, the following are also situated in this vicinity : Ballycar, the residence of Major John Colpoys ; Shepperton, of Jno. Gabbutt, Esq. ; Ralahine, of J. S. Vandeleur, Esq. ; Caherbane, of Jas. Creagh, Esq.; Carrigeary, of Major Creagh ; and Finloe, or Finlough, of H. P. Hickman, Esq., situated on the lake of that name. The parish is in the diocese of Killaloe ; part of the rectory was episcopally united, in 1802, to those of Kilnasoolagh, Kilconry, Kilmaleery, Clonloghan, Dromline, Finogh, and Bunratty, together constiuting the rectorial union of Tradree or Traddery, also called the union of Tomfinlogh, and in the patronage of the Earl of Egremont ; the remainder of the rectory is appropriate to the bishop's mensal : the vicarage forms part of the union of Kilfinaghty. The tithes amount to £142. 14. 7., of which £61. 16. 03/4. is payable to the rector, £30. 18. 61/4. to the vicar, and the remainder to the bishop ; the gross tithes of the rectorial benefice amount to £678. 14. 61/4. Adjoining the ruins of the old church is glebe of 23/4 acres. In the R. C. divisions the parish forms part of the union or district of Newmarket : the chapel, a spacious building, is situated in the town. About 400 children are educated in the public and private schools of the parish, of which that at Ballycar is under the patronage of Major Colpoys, aided by a grant from the Baptist society. At Newmarket is an embroidery school, under the patronage of Lady O'Brien, also a school supported by Mrs. Studder, and a society of Ladies. A large school-house has been lately built in the town by Sir Edw. O'Brien, by whom the school, which will be placed under the National Board of Education, will be supported. The old castle of Ralahine still exists ; and on Mohawn Hill is an ancient fort or rath of considerable dimensions.

TOMGRANEY, or **TOMGRENEI**, a parish, in the barony of **TULLA**, county of **CLARE**, and province of **MUNSTER** ; containing, with the post-town of Scariff, and the village of Tomgraney, 5568 inhabitants, of which number, 400 are in the village. An abbey was founded here in the earliest age of Christianity in Ireland, and flourished for many centuries : in 886 and 994 it was plundered. The church and steeple were rebuilt in 964 by the venerable Cormac O'Killeen, abbot of this house as well as that of Roscommon, and both abbot and bishop of Clonmacnois. In 1027 the steeple is said to have been again rebuilt by the great Brien Boroimhe, but in 1084 the abbey was reduced to ashes by O'Rourke of Breffny, who was, however, overtaken and slain by the men of this county. In 1164 it was again destroyed, and after being rebuilt was plundered about the year 1170. The only ancient ecclesiastical building now existing is the parish church, which is in the Norman style of architecture. The parish is situated on the river and bay of Scariff, opening into Lough Derg on the Shannon, and on the new line of road from Killaloe to Portumna, constructed chiefly along the shores of the lough. It comprises 7779 statute acres ; the land is in general excellent, and the soil in the vicinity of Scariff consists of limestone shale ; limestone and granite abound, and there is a considerable portion or reclaimable bog : the state of agriculture has been much improved. Great facility of communication with Dublin and Limerick is afforded by the vessels of the Inland Steam Navigation Company, which ply daily between those places. Fairs are held at the village on March 17th, May 17th, June 2nd, and Oct. 10th ; and petty sessions on alternate Fridays : a court for the manor of Raheens is also held there once a fortnight. The seats are Raheens, that of the Rev. Thos. B. Brady, abounding with fine timber and well stocked with deer ; Drewsborough House, of Fras. Drew, Esq. ; Ballyvannon House, of Lord Dunboyne ; and Shannon View, of M. Reddan, Esq. ; all commanding most interesting views of Lough Derg and the surrounding scenery. The living is a rectory, in the diocese of Killaloe, held from time immemorial with one-third part of the rectory of Kilballyhone, together constituting the corps of the prebend of Tomgraney, in the patronage of the Rev. Thos. B. Brady, the present incumbent. The tithes amount to £415. 7. 8$_{1/2}$., and, including the portion of Kilballyhone, to £498. 9. 3. The glebe comprises 11*a*. 2*r*. 23*p*. ; the glebe-house was built in 1814, when the late Board of First Fruits gave £100 and lent £1500 for its erection. The ancient church, a small building without a tower, has been lately repaired and improved, the Ecclesiastical Commissioners having granted £124 for that purpose. In the R. C. divisions the south-western portion of the parish forms the head of the district of Tomgraney, which also includes the parish of Kilnoe ; and the north-eastern portion forms the head of the district of Scariff, which also comprises the parish of Moynoe. In the former district are the chapels of Tomgraney and Bodike, and in the latter, those of Scariff and Knock-O'Grady : the chapel of Bodike is in the parish of Kilnoe, and the three others are in this parish. About 90 children are educated in two private schools. At Tomgraney are the remains of an old castle, and nearly in the centre of the village rises a singularly shaped rock. Lead ore exists in the vicinity, but it has not been worked ; and at Ballymalone is a chalybeate spring.

TRADDERY.-See **TOMFINLOE.**

TULLA, or **TULLOH**, a market and post-town, and a parish, in the barony of **TULLA**, county of **CLARE**, and province of **MUNSTER**, 10 miles (E.) from Ennis, and 109¾ (W. N. W.) from Dublin, on the road from Ennis to Killaloe ; containing 7514 inhabitants, of which number, 874 are in the town. This place appears to have some claims to antiquity ; there are numerous remains of ancient castles, formerly the residences of its landed proprietors. The town is pleasantly situated on a hill, and is surrounded with highly interesting scenery, enlivened with numerous elegant seats and pleasing villas. The principal trade is derived from its situation on a public thoroughfare, and is chiefly confined to the supply of the surrounding neighbourhood. The market is on Thursday ; fairs, chiefly for the sale of cattle, are held on May 13th and Sept. 29th. A chief constabulary police force is stationed in the town ; road sessions for the barony are held here, as are also petty sessions on alternate Thursdays, and a manorial court every month : there is a small bridewell for the district. The parish comprises 15,304 statute acres ; there is a large tract of mountain, and a considerable portion of bog ; the system of agriculture is rapidly improving ; the only waste land is mountain, which, in consequence of the improved lines of road now in progress, and the abundance of limestone, will be speedily reclaimed and brought into cultivation. On the ploughland of Mill-town is a lead mine, which was formerly worked but is at present discontinued ; and among the grey limestone rocks is a vein of white calcareous spar, which has not yet been worked. The principal seats are Maryfort, the residence of G. O'Callaghan, Esq. ; Kiltanon, of J. Moloney, Esq. ; Newlawn, of H. Westropp, Esq. ; Fort Anne, of J. Westropp, Esq. ; Cragg, of J. Maloney, Esq. ; Kilgoray, of D. O'Connell, Esq. ; Stone Hall, of T. McMahon, Esq. ; Knockane, of J. McMahon, Esq. ; Newgrove, of T. Browne, Esq. ; Tyredagh, of Mrs. Browne ; and Deremore, of F. Gore, Esq.

The living is a rectory and vicarage, in the diocese of Killaloe ; one moiety of the rectory forms part of the union of Ogashin, and the other, with the vicarage, constitutes the corps of the prebend of Tulloh in the cathedral of Killaloe. The tithes amount to £380. 15. 5¼., of which £284. 9. 11. is payable to the prebendary of Tulloh, £92. 6. 1¾ to the incumbent of Ogashin, and £3. 19. 4½.

to the prebendary of Tomgraney. The glebe-house is a good residence near the church, and the glebe comprises 2 3/4 acres ; the church, towards the erection of which the late Board of First Fruits granted a loan of £500, in 1812, is a neat edifice with a spire. The R. C. parish is co-extensive with that of the Established Church ; it contains two chapels, one in the town and one at Drimcharley. There are five private schools, in which are about 340 children ; and a dispensary. At Kiltanon is a succession of limestone caverns, through which a rivulet takes its course ; these are much visited in summer : many petrified shells are found in the limestone, some of which are nearly perfect and very curious. On the hill of Tulla are the remains of an ancient abbey, and of a druidical altar.

APPENDIX

ENNIS.
From the Clareen Bridge, in a straight Line in a South-westerly
Direction, to the Point at which the Road round the Hill from
Inch Bridge meets the Road to the Hermitage ; thence along a Bye
Road which runs Southward from the Point last described to the
Point (about Two hundred and twenty Yards from the Point last
described) at which such Bye Road is met by an Orchard Wall ;
thence in a straight Line to the Eastern Pier of a Gate on the Inch
Bridge Road which is the Entrance to Mr. Crow's Farm ; thence in
a straight Line to the Eastern Pier of a Gate on the Kilrush Road
about Two hundred and thirty Yards to the East of the Point at
which a Road branches from the Kilrush Road to join the Inch
Bridge Road ; thence in a straight Line in a South-easterly
Direction to the South-western Corner of Mr. Healy's Garden ;
thence along the Southern Wall of the same Garden to the Point at
which the same meets the Clare Road ; thence, Northward and
Eastward, along the Mail Coach Road from Clare (for about
Three Quarters of a Mile) to the Point at which the same is met by
a Wall on the Northern Side thereof near a Well ; thence in a
straight Line to the North-western Corner of the Wall which
surrounds a Distillery on the Banks of the River Fergus, but not
now in use ; thence along the last-mentioned Wall, including the
Distillery, to the Point at which the same Wall meets the River
Fergus ; thence in a straight Line in a North-easterly Direction to
the Point at which the Spancel Hill or Southern Gort Road is
joined by a Cross Road from the Northern Gort Road, and which
Point is distant about Four hundred Yards from the Bridge over
the River Fergus ; thence along the last-mentioned Cross Road to
the Point at which the same joins the Northern Gort Road ; thence
along the same Northern Gort Road for twenty-five Yards
beyond the Point last described ; thence in a straight Line in a
North-westerly Direction to the Windmill Stump ; thence in a
straight Line to the Clareen Bridge.

abbeys 1, 45, 53-4
Abbey 1
Abbyville House 37
Abhuinn O'Gearna 119
Acres 82
Adamson, Rev. W. 37
Adare 86
Adelphi House 92, 117
Agricultural Bank 43, 97-8
agriculture 17-19
Anchorite's Tower 52
Anglo-Normans 11
Annacarriga 113
Annals of the Four Masters
  114
antiquities 69, 84
Applevale House 16, 117
Archdall 56
Ardnacrusha 95, 96
Ardsallis 2-3
  river 24
Ardskegh quarry 100
Arranview House 77
Arthur, Thomas (Ballyquin)
  79
Arthur, Thomas (Paradise)
  58
Ashline Park House 37
Athlunkard 95
Atlantic Lodge 67
Atlantic Hotel 106
Aughnish 3
  Point 3, 14, 114
Ayle House 48

Bale bar 9
Baley, Henry T. 31
Ballagh slates 21
Ballconree South 69
Ballinacally 3, 58
Ballintlea House 67

Bally-McDonnell 81
Ballyaline 77
Ballyallaben House 38
Ballyally House 96
Ballyartney House 61, 79
Ballybran church 114
Ballycar 121
Ballyconree 3
Ballycorig Castle 30
Ballycullen Castle 69
Ballycunneen chapel 39
Ballyea chapel 80
Ballygannor 25, 112
Ballygrennan House 109
Ballygriffy Castle 40
Ballyhickey 115
Ballykeale House 65
Ballykilty House 111
Ballykishen 25
Ballylane Lodge 61
Ballyliddane 67
Ballylisky 28
Ballymacrenan 101
Ballymalone 122
Ballymurphy Castle 112
Ballynacraggy 3-4
  Castle 4, 38
Ballynahince Castle 95
Ballynalacken 77
Ballyquin 79
Ballysheen church 69
Ballysheenmore 69
Ballytigue 86
Ballyvalley House 75
Ballyvaughan 4
Baltard 75, 76
banks 43, 97-8
Banroe Castle 112
Baptist Society 121
Barclay, Richard 61, 79
Barefield 96

Barntick 28
baronies 13
bathing places2, 3, 69-70, 97, 104, 106
batteries 54, 79
Bearnageehy 80
Beechpark House 37
Behagh 2, 4
Bellisle House 101
Belvoir 31
Bentley, J. 81, 100
Besborough House 78
Bindon, Burton 1, 2
Bindon, S. 101
Birchfield House 83
Bishop's Quarter 38
Blackhead 50
Blackwater river 24
Blood, Bindon 37
Blood, Bindon 70
Blood, Rev. F. 28, 34, 51
Blood, Fitzgerald 111
Blood, J. 115
Blood, M. 92
Blood, Thomas 117
Board of Customs 97
Board of Inland Navigation 23, 73
Board of Public Works 48, 60
boat-building 72
boats 22, 76
Bodike 94, 122
bog-wood 20
Borough, Lieutenant 107
Borough, Randal 99
borough boundary of Ennis 124-5
boroughs 13
Boucher, Major 112
Brewe, W.A. 117
breweries 42, 43

bridewells and gaols 13
Bridgeman, Hewitt 40
Bridgeman, T. 48
Brien Boroihme 11, 25, 52, 54, 121
  palace of 15
Broadford 5, 20, 100
Brookville House 37
Brown, J. 112
Brown & Stein distillery 77
Browne, Mrs. 123
Browne, Thomas 123
Buckingham, Duke of 38
Buckingham, Marquess of 118
Buncraggy House 28
Buneagh Lough 70
Bunnahow House 51
Bunratty 5-7, 12, 26
  barony 11, 14-15
  canal 100
  castle 5, 6
  parish 6-7
  Roads 6
Burke, J. 32
Burke Lough 84
Burkes 32, 84
Burnard, E. 95
Burrane House 78
Burren 21
  town 1, 7
  barony 11
  agriculture in 15, 18
  harbour 2
Burtons 34
Burton, Bindon 30, 35
Burton, Edward W. 92, 117
Burton, Lady 8
Bushy Island 52
Butler, Austin, 51
Butler, H. 68

Butler, Henry 49
Butler, James B. 51
Butler, Rev. Theobald 78
Butler, Sir Theobald 33-4
Butler, Rev. William 81
Butler, W. 51

Caherbane 120
Caher House 48
Cahircalla House 37
Cahir Castle 114
Cahircon 61, 63, 64
Cahirfeenich 82
Cahirgal 76, 105
Cahirmurphy 49
Cahirvane House 83
Callaghan's Mills 7, 31
Camden 10
canals 24, 48, 73, 100
Canny, D. 6
Canon Island 7-8, 60
Canons Regular of St.
  Augustine 8
Cape Lean 57
Cappa Castle 69
  Lodge 99
Carabane House 88
Caradole House 78
Carhue 40
Carne 9
Carnelly House 28
Carolan's receipt 41
Carrick-on-Oultagh 108
Carrigfoyle 54
Carrigaholt 8-9, 26, 57, 108
Carrigeary 83
  House 59
Carriginriree 60
Carrignagoule 70
  castle 71
Carrigorin House 90

Carroll, John 62
Carron 9-10
Carrune 9
Cassino 26, 106
Castlecoote, Lord 57, 67, 76
castles 26, 77, 81, 91
Castle Crine 68, 69
Castle Lake 68
Castle Fergus 36, 115
Castle Lough House 75
Castlepark House 109
Caswell, S. 95
Cathal, Prince of Connaught
  11
Cathiana 53
caves 46, 60, 69, 93, 124
Ceanchora 75
Cellumabrach 64
Charles II 49
cholera 37
Church of the Nuns 68
Cistertian abbeys 1
Clan Cuilean 11
Clancy, Boetius 77
Clare
  county of 10-27, 116
  Lord 8
  town 27-28
Clare-Abbey 28-9
Clarecastle 27-8
Clareen
  bridge 124, 125
  river 24
Clarefield 108
Clare Road, Ennis 124
Claresford 71
Clehansevan 57, 58
Clenagh Castle 83
Clifden House 117
Cliffs of Moher 15, 82
Clifton 63

130

Dunbeg 24, 39, 76
Dunlicky castle 108
Dunmore 57, 56
Dynish 56, 59
Dysert 25, 26, 39-41

East India fleet 64
Edenvale House 80
Edward I 11
Egremont, Earl of 35
Elanagranoch 8
electors 13, 43
Elm Hill 81
  House 101
Elmvale House 92
Enagh 31
Ennis 41-6
Ennis-Corker 33
Enniskerry 46
Ennistubret 60
Ennistymon 21, 22, 46-8, 114
  House 47, 84
  river 24
Enniskerry Island 15
Eocha Baildearg 71
Erasmus Smith Schools 44-5, 99
Erina House 101

Fairy Lawn House 112
Farahie Bay 67
Feacle 48-9
Fenabore 64
Fergus, River 24
Fermoyle 49
Ferriter, E. 68
Fidane castle 71
Fierd 58
Finerana school 114
Finogh 49-50
  House 121

Finucane, Andrew 47, 84
Finucane, Michael 36
Finucane family 61
Finvarra 50
  House 1
  Point 3, 14, 50, 114
fishing 1-2, 4, 5, 7, 8, 22, 57, 67, 72, 73, 75-6, 77, 92, 97, 101, 104, 104, 107
  see also oyster fishing
Fishery Board 2, 8, 39, 57, 97
Fitzgerald, F. 92
Fitzgerald, Mrs. 65
Fitzgerald, Sir William 84, 90, 111
Fitzgerald, William 92
Fitzgerald family 91
Fitzgerald and Vesci, Lord 36, 51, 115, 117
Fitzgibbon family 27
Flaithbeartach 54
Flower, Captain 115
Fodera Hill 58
forestry 19, 48
Fort Anne 123
Foyne's Island 64
Fort Fergus 58
Foster, J 70
Fountain 40
Franciscan friars 114
Freagh 106
  castle 63
freeholders 13
Fuhers Lodge 112
Furnace-town 48
Furness 32
  abbey 1
Fynish 50, 56, 59

Gabbett, John 68
Gabbutt, Jno. 120

Inchioveagh 103
Inchiquin
  Baron 12
  barony 11, 14-15
  castle 92
  lake 91
Inchmore 35
industry 111, 118
Inis-Cathay 53
Inis-Cronan 51
Inis-fidhe 56
Inisluaidhe penitentiary 61
Inland Steam Navigation
  Co. 122
Inniscalthra (parish) 52-3
Inniscalthra (Island) 25, 52
Inniscattery 11, 53-5
Inniscluanruadha 41
Innisdadrom 55-6
Innisherk 60
Innislaunaght abbey 1
Innismacnaughten 56, 59
Innismore 58
Innisneganananagh 7-8
Irish language 26
Islands(Barony) 15
Island of the Seven
  Churches 52
Island of the Starved Bishop
  68
Isle Ruagh 59
Ivers, W. 68

James, J. 28

Kane, Captain Richard 95
Keane, F. 37, 54, 55
Keane, R. 37
Keane, W. 37
Kelly, J. 67
Kilbaha 56-7

Kilballyhone 57-8
Kilbane chapel 100
Kilbarron 48
Kilcarragh 66
Kilchrist 58-9, 61
Kilcleran 49
Kilclogher headland 57
Kilconry 59
Kilcorney 59-60
Kilcredane Point 20
Kildysart 59, 60-61
Kilfarboy 61-3
Kilfedane 63-4
Kilfenora 15, 25, 64-6
  diocese 13, 64-5, 101
Kilfentinan 66-7
Kilfieragh 67-8
Kilfinaghty 68-9
Kilforbrick 62
Kilgoray House 123
Kilheny 59, 69
Kilgorey House 95
Kilkadrane 107
Kilkee 67, 68, 69-70, 105
Kilkeedy 70
Kilkeedy castle 71
Kilkerin 79
Kilkishen 26, 31, 71, 90
Kill-da Lua 71
Killaloe 23, 25, 71-5
  diocese 13, 73-5
  slates 20
Killanna 79
Killard 75-6
Killaspuglenane 76
Killeany 76
Killeely 77-8
Killeilagh 77
Killenana 49
Killeely 109
Killeymur 78-9

Liscanor 104-105
Lisdeen 67, 68, 105
Lisdoonvarna 26, 86, 87
livestock 18, 19, 69, 86
Lloyd, G. 102
Lloyd, T. 79
Lloyd, William 111
Lobdell, C. 70
local government 13, 43
Loghans 16
Lord Clare's pier 9
Loughnamina 62, 63
Loughrask 105
Low Island 60, 61
Lucas, Dr. Charles 93
Lucas family 84
Ludlow, General 8
Lysaght, George F. 84
Lysaght, James 101
Lysaght family 65
Lyssane quarry 100

Mac Adgail, Donmhall 75
Mac Brodie 27
Mac Curtin 41
Mac Mahon, Rev. Dr. 115
Mac Mahon, Teigue Keigh 8
Mac Mahon family 8, 12, 83, 108
Mac Maoilnamba, Diarmuid 54
Mac Namara, Macon Dall 114
Mac Namara, Sioda Cam 114
Mac Namara family 11, 26, 115, 117
Madden, Mr. 44
Magowna House 94
Mahon, Charles 37
Mahon, H. 101

Mahon, J. 37
Mahon, Robert 37
Mahon, Thomas 37
Mahre 26
  castle 40
Mail Coach road, Ennis 124
Malbay 15, 89
Manby, Captain 9
Mansell, Edward 50
market-towns 13
martello towers 3, 50, 114
Martin, Francis 118
Martin, Rev. J. 88
Maryfort House 123
Massey, H. 101
Massey, Lady 102
Massey, Sir Hugh Dillon 101
Mc Adam, P. 95
Mc Curtin, Hugh 34
Mc Donnell, J. (Kilkee House) 67
Mc Donnell, J. (New Hall) 80
Mc Grath, E. 48
Mc Inerney, Rev. T. 49
Mc Mahon J. 123
Mc Mahon, Patrick 32
Mc Mahon, Rev. Dr. 36
Mc Mahon, Sir Teigue 89
Mc Mahon, Thomas 59
Mc Mahon, W. 66
Mc Namara, Francis 77
Mc Namara, G. 38
Mc Namara, J. 48
Mc Namara, J. 83
Mc Namara, Mathew 41
Mc Namara, Major William N. 77
Meelick 77
Meelick House 32
members of parliament 13
Merville Lodge 62

Ross
  House 112
  glebe 113
Ross Hill House 61
Rossmanaher 49
Rossroe castle 90
Roughan, J. 70
round towers 25
Roxton House 117
Ruan 40
Runnard House 102
Ryhinch House 75

Saints' Island 6
Sampson, D. 94
Sans Souci House 38
Sarsfield, Patrick 72
Scariff 118-119, 121
  chapel 122
Scarlets 66
Scart 31
Scattery Island 25
Scott, Bindon 58, 60, 61, 63,
  79
Scott, John 29, 85
Scott, William 115
Seafield 89
Seaview House 62
Shallee castle 94
Shally 16
Shanahea 63
Shannon river 23-4
Shannon Steam Navigation
  Co. 72-3
Shene Hill 119
Shepperton House 120
shipping 2, 6, 7, 73, 88, 90,
97, 103, 106, 122
shooting 5, 79, 86
Sidney, Sir Henry 12
Singleton, Hugh 115

Singleton, John 115
Siol Gangain 10
Sion Ville 31
Six-Mile-Bridge 119-120
Skerret, William J. 1
Slaney 80
Slievedooly 79
Slieveilva 86
smelting 118
Smith, William 115
Smithstown 26
  castle 39, 101
Smithwick, William 75
Smyth, Bishop 110
Smyth, Richard 109
soil 16-17
South Sound 77
Spaight, T. 79
spa waters 26
Spancel Hill
  road, Ennis 125
  school 30
Spanish Armada 62, 82, 106
Spanish Point 62, 106
Springfield House 50, 68,
  101
Spring Hill House 95
St. Aidan 54
St. Bridget's
  nunnery 56
  holy well 83
St. Caimin 52
St. Catherine's House 94
St. Coelan 52
St. Columb 10
St. Cosgrath 52
St. Fachnan 64, 65, 73
  church of 10
St. John's Well 80
St. Kieran 54
St. Lelia's chapel 109

Tulla 123
 barony 11, 14
Tullagower 98
Tulloh 123
Tullynaglashin 25
Tuoreem House 36
Turloghmore 16
Turlough castle 114
turloughs 16
Turraghmore 70
Tuthill, J. 95
Twiss, Captain 112
Tyredagh House 123
Ulster, Earl of 12
Ulster Man's Rock 108
Urlin castle 83
Ursuline Convent, Ennis 44

Vandeluer, Crofton M. 97,
 98, 99, 100
Vandeluer J. S. 120
Vanhoogart, Mr. 107
Villiers, Hannah 110
Violet Hill House 100
Vincent, G. 101

Walker, C. 100
Walsh, A. 102
Walsh, Captain J. 102
Walsh, Rev. S. 34, 92
Ware, Rev. James 11
Waterpark House 101
Wellesley Bridge 109
Well Park House 36, 115
Western Corkavaskin 8
Westpark House 62
Westrop, Ralph 94
Westrop, Rev. T. 102
Westropp, H. 123
Westropp, J. 123
Westropp, Rev. J. 38

Westropp, Thomas 112, 113
Whitehall 95
White Strand, Moyarta 107
Whitty, Archdeacon 47, 84
Willbrook House 117
Willow Bank House 37
Wilson, D. 31
Wilson, E. 50
windmill stump, Ennis 125
Woodfield House 100
Woodlawn House 88
Woodmount House 84
Wood-Park House 6, 53
Woodthorp chapel 109

Yellow Dragoons 8
Youghall House 75

445